Praise for

"Congrats on the book and y
for you! This is really a big (
get your words!"

BOB GOFF, author of the New York Times Best-Selling book
Love Does: Discover a Secretly Incredible Life in an Ordinary World

"Dave has a special knack for storytelling. He is able to capture beautiful imagery with his words and inspire others with his contagious joy. Hope radiates off the pages of this book-both in the stories that had me laughing loudly, and in the stories I had to grab a few tissues for. Hope Has Arrived will encourage readers to intentionally live life in the abundance of love and grace we were meant to."

KENDRA BROEKHUIS, author of *Here Goes Nothing: An
Introvert's Reckless Attempt to Love Her Neighbors*

"Dave Kinsman combines sage wisdom with a childlike joy in *Hope Has Arrived*. The mixture is uplifting yet reflective, celebratory yet guiding, and will leave you ready to embrace the life God intended for you!"

KYLE WILLKOM, Founder, Action Packed Leadership,
Author of *Wake Up Call and The Thinking Dilemma*

"Everyone needs to read this book. It's inspiring, uplifting and encouraging. It invites you to more intimacy with God, honesty with yourself while empowering you to grow in ways you never knew possible."

LANCE EDWARD, Founder, Ministry Arts Academy,
Author of *The Undeniable Experience*

"After reading a chapter in *Hope Has Arrived*, I wanted to continue my journey onto the next adventure in this captivating book. Dave has a way of story telling which makes a person feel as if they were on the journey themselves. Dave is an inspiration"

LISA FAHEY, Author of *Rise Up, Women of God*
and Simply a Study on Ecclesiastes

"Dave Kinsman's home spun stories capture the essence of hope. An enjoyable read!"

DR. RALPH W. NEIGHBOR, III, Associate Pastor Mosaic LA

"Witty, engaging and so uplifting...that's what Dave has so brilliantly crafted in *Hope Has Arrived*. The humorous and heartfelt stories have left me with a renewed desire to seek the face of Jesus in a new and exciting way!"

KATHY LESNAR, Co-founder/ President All Day Fore Africa, Inc.

HOPE
HAS ARRIVED

Embracing the Hope
That Lies Within

DAVE KINSMAN

WESTBOW
PRESS®
A DIVISION OF THOMAS NELSON
& ZONDERVAN

Author photo by: Visual Image Photography, Cedarburg, WI

WestBow Press books may be ordered through booksellers or by contacting:

WestBow Press
A Division of Thomas Nelson & Zondervan
1663 Liberty Drive
Bloomington, IN 47403
www.westbowpress.com
1 (866) 928-1240

ISBN: 978-1-9736-1237-7 (sc)
ISBN: 978-1-9736-1238-4 (hc)
ISBN: 978-1-9736-1236-0 (e)

Library of Congress Control Number: 2017919642

Print information available on the last page.

WestBow Press rev. date: 01/25/2018

CONTENTS

ACKNOWLEDGMENTS

You, a vast cast of characters, have inspired me to create the narrative of this book. Some of you have been named, and others, no less important to me, remain unnamed. All of you are equally vital to the life of these pages. You have influenced me and encouraged me to give words to the stories that will be unleashed into our world. Your voice, your inspiration, your passion are intertwined throughout the pages of this book.

Thank you to my Sweetie Dawn, whose sacrifice and love has made all the difference in the world in bringing this book to completion. Thanks also to my sons Josh, Jonny, Zach, Nathan and Ben, for your encouragement throughout this last year. Patience was required and there is nothing like having your greatest fans within your own family. You've brought about some the most memorable stories!

King Author would like to thank the Knights of the Round Table! The coffee klatsch crew from Fiddleheads: John and his St. Bernard Buddy and Tori his Greyhound, Gordon, Chip, Chuck and Kenny; the baristas, Ashley, Sarah and Hannah, who have kept me on point throughout this past year of writing and allowing me to have the most beautiful scenery in which to write this book. It was a game changer!

To Team Catalyst: Nino, Amy, Mark, Katie, Joe, Kaitlyn and Mike. Your selfless commitment is a testament to your friendship and leadership. Thanks for partnering with me in this endeavor.

I couldn't have achieved the end game without you taking this journey with me. I am so proud of you guys! Thanks for helping me achieve a reality that once was a dream!

Finally, I would like to thank all the cast of characters who have created the backdrop of this book. I'm profoundly grateful for my parents, Earle and Constance, whose love has been so instrumental. Many thanks also to the authors who have changed how I look at life: Henry Nouwen, Erwin McManus, Bob Goff and Mother Theresa, just to name a few.

To my dearest friends, thank you! It is a privilege to have journeyed with you these past thirty years. You know who you are! Each of you has revealed glimpses of who God is. You have also given me the material with which to create stories that are a part of the fabric of who I am.

Thank you, Nikki Mata and all of you at WestBow Press for seeing this project through to completion. I am excited to finish what I started!

Most importantly, I thank God for the opportunity to love a whole lot of people over the span of my life. Love is truly the end game of our journey!

1

BROOKS

My life has always been one adventure of uncertainty after another. There is something amazing about saying yes to uncertainty. It drives one to trust. It allows room for the divine, a companion you sense is there or at least *hope* is there when you've decided to go all in on life-changing decisions. These are decisions that won't simply affect one's personal life, but the lives of those who have been entrusted to us as well.

It's the summer of 1988, and I've just moved from St. Paul, Minnesota. To some, it may seem that my new hometown is out in the middle of nowhere, as in smack-dab in the middle of the South Dakota plains. Pierre, South Dakota, to be exact, is a city nestled along the beautiful bluffs of the Missouri River. This is a place where stories and friendships will unfold over a lifetime.

On the day I'm calling to mind, it's a beautiful summer afternoon. A gentle, cool breeze hints that our days of summer are coming to a close. I just have to say it. I love summer! Everything in creation is bursting with color, fragrance, and beauty. There's also a deep sense of wanting to slow down and appreciate each day because before too long it will be time to transition into a new South Dakota season. It's on one of these special end-of-summer days that my life and the life of a total stranger changed forever.

On that Monday afternoon, I practically have the entire beach to myself. It's my day off, so to speak. All I could think is, *What a gift to be out here along the banks of this tranquil yet powerful river!* So not wasting any time, I decide to do some lap swimming from buoy to buoy, roughly a twenty-five meter swim.

I love swimming nearly as much as I love summer. There is something uniquely peaceful about moving through water. It's life without any interruptions. For me, it also means uninterrupted prayer. The words I pray while swimming are never audible, but my heart is near bursting in expression.

This particular day, I am praying for a specific person. I can't seem to identify a familiar face or voice to help me recognize who it is. All I can say is that I am crying out to God on behalf of someone I've never met before, but a person who desperately needs prayer. The prayer comes to an end at the same time as my energy, so I tuck my toes down into the squishy river bottom and trudge back to shore. The beach is definitely calling me to take up residence and enjoy one of the last warm days of the season.

I shake my towel free of vagrant pebbles, and pleasantly exhausted, stretch out on it. No sooner do I lay my head back and feel the heat of sunshine on my skin when thoughts of my swim start zipping through my brain. Instantly I'm acutely aware of everything around me, as if the world is now a slow-motion film. Then I hear the scream, what sounds like the high-pitched, broken scream of an adolescent boy.

I think, *Aw, c'mon! Here I am trying to enjoy one of my only days off. It happens to be gorgeous out, and now this? But what is this?*

I look down the beach toward some commotion on the dock about fifty yards away and sense something is seriously wrong. Instantly alarmed and alert, I start sprinting toward the chaos.

An inconsolable woman is screeching, "Brooks! Brooks!"

Stepping out onto the dock above the water, I see a group of men with sagging shoulders of defeat and resignation. They're just standing there on the dock around a tiny body. Their faces are pale

2

and hopeless. Their hearts are deflated. I lock eyes with an older gentleman hovering closely over the lifeless little boy.

"What happened?" I ask him.

He tells me that they found the child trapped under the dock, face-down in the water. They have already checked his vitals and found no pulse, and his eyes are rolled back. They can't tell me how long he was underwater. The men are paralyzed with grief and what must have been deep sadness in their inability to resuscitate the tiny victim.

At our feet is the precious body of a boy named Brooks. I'm looking at a lifeless three-year-old little boy, unwilling to accept that he is dead. Kneeling close beside him, I put my hands on his small forehead and begin to pray firmly and loudly, believing hope will arrive. As I am praying for Brooks, I recall a movie I recently caught on TV, including a scene of a lifeguard using lifesaving techniques to help a boat crash victim.

Intensely focused in this present moment, I look up from my kneeling position near Brooks to the man who is closest and directly across from me. (I will find out later he is Brooks' grandfather.) With an authority I didn't know I possessed, I guide him through the very same lifesaving measures I had just seen on TV. Now, I know full well that I am ill equipped and untrained, but these men need the hope I'm offering. Uncertainty visibly starts to fade and instead turns into bold strength.

I feel Brooks' heart crying out. His words, like my prayers in the water, are not audible, but they are identifiable. After what seems like an eternity, but actually only minutes, Brooks convulses and gags, and a gush of river water spurts up from his nose and mouth. It's his nonverbal declaration that he is in the fight, the battle for one more breath, one more moment, and one more day.

Searing through the miracle unfolding before us is the siren of an approaching ambulance. All of a sudden, Brooks begins to cry. I lift up his limp, worn-out, little body, and our group races from

3

the dock to meet arriving EMTs. They expertly assess Brooks and fasten him on the stretcher, and they are underway to the hospital.

I don't want to part ways with Brooks' family as fear-filled as they are, so I join the caravan rushing to the ER. Together we sit and pray in the hospital waiting room for an agonizing amount of time. I'm clinging to the hope that I'll have one more opportunity to see Brooks.

At last, he's stabilized enough for visitors, and I'm standing at the end of his recovery room bed. Just while I'm thinking that he's such a tiny, frail person in a huge, oversized bed, we lock gazes. No words are said, and none are needed. Brooks' face is, without any doubt whatsoever, the exact face I envisioned during my prayer laps between the river buoys. I'm now standing next the very person who came to mind as I was swimming that day. This is the soul I never knew, the voice I never heard until today.

I'm convinced that this story is life changing not only for Brooks, his family, and me, but maybe for you as well. Perhaps you're drowning in what you think is your own insignificance. You're drowning in what you see as your inability to grasp dreams that seem so elusive, wondering why others seem to have all the luck.

Know that there is a voice that penetrates the chaos and is calling out your name. This voice cries out, encouraging you to take just one more breath. This voice knows one more breath will lead to life.

Brooks is now a young man in his later twenties. He has given his life to saving people, individuals he has never met with faces he has never seen and will likely never see again. Very fittingly, Brooks is now a firefighter and EMT. He has decided to give back what was nearly taken from his some twenty-five years prior along the banks of the Missouri River, life!

Each of us is entrusted with a story, a narrative that calls us to breathe life into those who are drowning. Through a life-giving narrative, others might encounter a powerful voice and persuasive presence calling them to once again breathe.

QUESTIONS TO PONDER

1. Maybe you're one prayer away from a life being saved. Sometimes the size of our prayer is in direct proportion to the size of our God. Do you pray for the impossible?

2. What might you be drowning in? What does God need to rescue you from?

3. Who in your circle of influence can you breathe life into today? Maybe, just maybe, it's a matter of life and death.

2

BETTER TOGETHER

How else could I possibly start this story than by simply plunking you down with me in the middle of an elementary school classroom a long time ago?

Three other fifth graders and I were sitting on desks in an empty classroom, waiting to have our guitar lesson with Sister Kay. A huge green chalkboard on the front wall was half erased, and we could still see clouds of chalk bits floating around in the late afternoon sun. The room smelled like wood shavings from the crank pencil sharpener screwed into the wall by the door. It was just an ordinary schoolroom until Sister Kay came in.

Sister certainly embodied the personality of a singing nun. She had a boisterous, joyful laughter that sometimes sounded like a machine gun firing rounds. She especially seemed to laugh during our guitar lessons. We didn't even feel bad about that. It was the total opposite actually. Her laughter brought a calm to us, who were feeling anxious and inadequate about our guitar playing.

Even though the four of us were about as different from each other as we could be, Sister Kay had a gift of bringing out what was best and most unique in each of us. Our guitar group consisted of Todd, a tall, lanky kid who simply had a knack for playing and learning his music; Tim, a bit of a rebel with no other cause than to create disturbances in our fifth-grade classroom; and Doug, the heartthrob of the fifth-grade class. As a matter of fact, Doug could play a song with all the wrong chords and still make the girls cry.

Then there was me. I got along with everybody and didn't make trouble, but I had a hurdle ahead of me in trying to learn guitar. You see, I was missing about an inch of my middle finger. What seemed so easy for the other kids in the guitar group was tough for me to learn.

When I was around three years old, our elderly babysitter accidentally slammed the door on my finger. (Let's just say "Ouch!")

With a certain presence of mind, the babysitter called my Aunt Ginny instead of 9-1-1 because her husband, my Uncle Jerry, was a doctor. In a panic, Aunt Ginny drove over to our home, packed me up, and rushed me off to the emergency room, only to have Uncle Jerry ask her, "Where's the rest of it?"

Aunt Ginny had no other choice but to rush back to my house to collect the rest of my finger in hopes that it could be reattached. Well, to make a long story short (or a finger even shorter), the reattachment didn't work out. And there began the challenge of my overcoming a sense of feeling flawed.

Way back when, Sister Kay saw each of her guitar students for the people they could potentially be. To me, she brought a garland of courage to replace the yoke of inadequacy I'd been hauling around. Her constant love and care chiseled away at what I thought were my imperfections. She saw possibility where I saw limitations.

In fact, Sister Kay produced such a confidence in me that, all these many years later, I continue to play guitar. It's beyond playing really. I have a great passion for leading worship and have been able to instill in many others the same love for music that Sister Kay instilled in me. I allowed that joy-filled, humble nun to meet me in the place where I was most vulnerable. I permitted her to help me overcome fear and leaned on her through the learning journey to success.

It's become clear to me now that dreams and aspirations are best achieved when we allow others to take the journey with us, when we let others really know us before we have it all figured out. We can allow people to encourage or challenge us, according to our need. It's always better together than alone!

Isn't it strange how experiences become generational? I mean, Sister Kay taught me guitar and how not to compare myself with others and helped me grow beyond difficult circumstances. Then many years later, I had a unique and unexpected opportunity to pay it forward.

I wasn't too far into my first big ministry position as a church youth pastor as this story unfolded. On a particular Saturday evening, I was leading a retreat for about fifty middle-school students. During a dramatic skit that my team and I were performing, two high school students walked into the church and seated themselves way in the back. I thought to myself, *Now that's a bit odd.*

As soon as I broke away and walked toward them, I realized that one of the two latecomers was doubled over and weeping uncontrollably. Together with another member of my team and through many tears, we learned that one of the teenagers, Lance, had been breaking under the weight of all his challenges: divorce, remarriages, stepparents, unacceptable behavior, suspension, expulsion, foster care, and more expulsion. His hopes for this life were diminishing right before his eyes … until that very night. That night, one of his friends cared enough to drive him to where they knew a retreat was happening. That evening, hope arrived.

Only a few days after the lifesaving retreat, Lance's mother asked if I'd be willing to take on guardianship and allow him to live with me for a while. Without much hesitation, I agreed.

And just after, my brain kicked in. I thought, *I'm a single twenty-eight-year-old, and I'm going to raise a teenage kid? What am I doing? I'm clueless!*

Yet here on my doorstep was a desperate mother who saw something in me that perhaps I didn't even see in myself at the time. Maybe, just maybe, I had something to offer that teenage boy after all.

Lance arrived at my apartment with all he owned in the world: one suitcase of clothes, a sleeping bag, some blankets, a pillow, and a fan. I was tempted to be like the innkeeper proclaiming to Mary and Joseph, "There's no room at the inn!"

But I asked myself, "What would love do?" and proceeded to get him settled in. My former living room was transformed into a teenager's bedroom, and it would be so for over a year.

In the dead of winter, I finally had to cave in and ask Lance why on earth he ran his fan every night.

He looked at me. "The fan's white noise brings me comfort so I don't feel alone. It helps me fall asleep."

The word "comfort" gave voice to a need for belonging, a sense of home, and a feeling of peace, even when the world was hurling all its difficulties his way.

Over time, Lance and I began to realize that we actually had quite a lot in common. Both of us are a little bit ADD, maybe one more than the other. (And it's not Lance.)

We discovered that we both had a deep appreciation for music. Lance was a gifted writer and shared numerous poems he penned to help him through tough days. I asked if he'd ever thought about putting his poems to music. Not playing an instrument, he thought it would be nice someday.

In that very moment, I remembered the life lessons that Sister Kay taught me in fifth grade. It was almost as if everything she helped me through back then was to prepare me for that future day with Lance. On that day, we two would embark on a journey of discovery.

For Lance, it was a discovery of unearthing all the songs and narratives of his life. For me, it was a process of learning how to love and trust a kid who considered himself to be unlovable and unforgivable. It was a process of patiently listening to the stories of his heart, one filled with insecurities and anxieties. I learned to really listen to a teenager who longed to have worth and identity and wanted to be part of something greater and lasting.

Lance's birthday was just around the corner, and I wanted to provide a gift for him that would help him express all of those emotions penned up inside this young man's heart. I bet you already guessed that I purchased him a guitar. I knew how much solace that instrument brought to my life, so why not share that same gift with Lance? It turns out that this gift produced beauty, laughter, and even some tears.

Then began his lessons, but not just guitar lessons. They were lessons about life, faith, and hope that would be interwoven throughout his songs. Lance continued to craft his voice and guitar-playing skills.

At one point, he finally asked why I didn't use my middle finger when I played. I told him the story of the babysitter, the door, and the feeling of inferiority. I told him that what I once thought was a handicap was actually a gift called determination, which helped me overcome my odds and actually excel beyond what I thought I could ever achieve. I told Lance the story about a sweet nun who believed in me when I didn't necessarily believe in myself.

I looked at Lance. "Kid, you have more talent in your pinky finger than others could ever hope for. But what you do with those gifts matters. You need to share those gifts not only within the confines of our little community, but with the world!"

And he did. He shared his gifts so much so that others came alongside him, invested in his talents, and gave him opportunities to share them. Lance was in Nashville working on an album, laying down some guitar tracks with a plethora of extremely influential musicians.

In the middle of a song, one of the well-known guitarists

stopped Lance to ask him, "Hey, man, why aren't you playing with that middle finger?"

Lance shrugged. "Well, the guy who taught me was missing part of his finger, so that's how I learned to play."

They all laughed at the thought. Here Lance had a perfectly functioning middle finger, yet didn't use its full potential when he performed.

Lance uncovered a huge life lesson that day: Life brings all sorts of challenges our way. Heaps of obstacles, both seen and unseen, can be placed in front of us. When we jump that fence of insecurity, we can craft a song or circumstance we would never have dreamed possible.

In order to jump, we need the strength shown to us through teachers, mentors, parents, a Sister Kay, a friend, or an overcomer, one who just might happen to be missing part of his middle finger.

QUESTIONS TO PONDER

1. Who had the most significance or impact in mentoring you?

2. Who do you envision pouring your time, faith, or resources into?

3. What fence of insecurity did you jump in order to accomplish your goal?

3

GALE FORCE WINDS

Most people abhor Mondays. It's usually the day to catch up on all of the previous week's unfinished business. It's the day of the week your coworkers tend to reveal their true selves.

At this point of my life, Mondays rocked, and my coworkers were convinced I was super dedicated. On Mondays, I knew that, if I put in the usual intense day at work and checked off each item on my to-do list, I'd be rewarded with my weekly co-ed pickup basketball game that evening.

I had some highly competitive friends at the attorney general's office. Our pickup basketball game more closely resembled a cross between tackle football and a three-ring circus. Let's just say that it was a way for all of us to leave our work behind at the office and take our stress out on the court. Maybe one out of every two of us playing actually possessed some skill or, maybe more importantly, proper basketball etiquette. We had fun anyway. Well, most of us.

The other players called me "Chairman of the Board," and I suppose there's a good reason for that. I had a particular fondness for the game of football and achieved some success in that sport. The thing is that I had a little bit of difficulty harnessing football's rough-and-tumble competitive spirit on a basketball court.

On one particular Monday evening, I might have gone a little too far. My good friend Rex was not necessarily the epitome of what you would call a honed athlete. At a glance, you might not even guess he enjoyed playing basketball as much as he did. Rex is an excellent lawyer, great actor, and dear friend, but not a threat on the court, if you know what I mean. Still, for whatever reason, his team captain always selected him to guard me. That's like "Hulk Hogan meets Richard Simmons."

When the ref blew his whistle, our point guard, Bridget, passed the ball to me, which I quickly passed on to Janine. Janine saw me driving toward the board and threw me an alley-oop to drop in the bucket for a score. Nothing was going to stand in the way of my making that perfect basket! I was so focused that I neglected to see Rex standing right in front of me, and I plowed into him, moving forward at full throttle. Rex smacked hard on the wooden court floor. The air was knocked out of him, and his glasses were broken and hanging off his face. I don't think he liked me too much right then.

Since our game was halted, I noticed the sound of my ringtone over on the team bench. Deciding that it gave me a chance to exit an awkward situation, I jogged over to answer the call. It was my bride of just a few months, Dawn.

She said, "Honey, your young adult group is meeting over at the church in a few minutes, and they were really hoping you planned to be there."

Have you ever had one of those days where you try to cram in just a little bit more than you were ever capable of accomplishing? That had already been my day, so I tried to come up with any sort of excuse to get me out of praying with the young adults. I was tired, hungry, and just not in the mind-set to pray, especially after my can-crush incident with Rex.

Ever the wise woman, my sweetie convinced me to man up and go.

I told her, "Babe, I smell, and I haven't had anything to eat."

She reminded me that there were couple of fast-food restaurants on the way to the gathering and I shouldn't be a wimp. So taking her advice, I ordered a couple of burritos at Taco John's drive-thru. I chugged a soft drink to wash them down and managed to arrive only a few minutes late.

As I entered the church, I saw about thirty young adults as well as five or so blue hairs in the front pew. Blue hairs are those women in your church who have been praying for you and the whole world over the past seventy-plus years, and every time they go to the salon, their grey hair gains an ever so slight tint of blue. (You don't mess with those prayer warrior gals either because they have a direct link with God Almighty.)

Not wanting to create any kind of disturbance, I quietly found a seat toward the back of the church. The sanctuary lights were set at dim, tall votive candles were lit, and the young adults' prayers were being voiced and heard.

I found myself lulled into a peaceful stupor. Tired and worn out from the day's exertions, I assumed the prayer position, kneeling with my bum nudging the seat of the pew and my hands and head resting on top of the pew in front of me.

That night, the group decided to pray a beautiful prayer during which one meditates on the life of Christ. The only thing about that form of prayer is that it's really calming and reflective. So much so that, if you're not mindful, it can draw you into a deep sleep. (If anyone knows this, it's me!)

Prayers continued. What happened next probably scarred the blue hairs for life. The combination of tiredness, Mexican food, and reflective prayer worked like a rumbling Molotov cocktail. I had fallen asleep, waking only when I realized that I broke wind. And not just any wind, it was the loudest gale force wind ever! It was seriously so loud that it woke me from a deep sleep. It didn't even occur to me at first that I was the culprit!

I was so stunned that it took a few moments before I remembered where I actually was. *Oh, yeah.*

Slowly I realized that the person leading the prayer could

barely speak. She was trying to get out the next words of the prayer without bursting into utter fits of laughter. I felt like the famous comedian, Chris Farley, who tried to cover his embarrassment by hiding his big, round self behind a light post! It was not going to happen.

I didn't know what on earth to do, so I just buried my head in a pious position, hunched myself further down into the pew, and fervently prayed, *Lord, forgive me, for I know not what I've done!* I figured that, if I just kept my face down long enough to regain my composure, no one would know where that gale force wind had come from.

After the final "Amen" and sign of the cross, the blue hairs prayerfully and quietly began filing out of their pew. Watching them walk toward me in the back, all I could think was, *Oh no! Here comes the secret service. I hope they don't know it was me!*

The last one of the blue hairs in the queue winked at me and chuckled as she passed by. Her joyful smile told me she definitely knew who the offender was.

As they exited out into the parking lot, a roar of unrestrained laughter filled the church. Every last one of the remaining young adults looked back at me and shouted, "Kinsman! What were you thinking?"

I explained, "I wasn't! I was sleeping, and I had two burritos too many tonight!"

* * *

I love what St Teresa of Calcutta said about joy, "Joy is a net of love by which we catch souls."[1] I have realized more and more over the past thirty years that joy has played such a significant role in my life. When worries, trials, and struggles overwhelm me, joy orients my heart back to the author and source of all joy.

---

[1] Mother Teresa of Calcutta (1997 St. Teresa of Calcutta), Missionaries of Charity, 1981 Calendar Writings.

The virtue of joy is not something you can simply muster up. It's a disposition of the heart. It is a decision. Once you choose joy, however, you'll find healing in your heart, mind, and soul.

Do you recall the last time you laughed so hard that you had tears rolling down your face, you couldn't catch a breath, and you were doubled over holding your belly, wishing for a bathroom? Choosing joy has brought about the most healing and hope in my own life. It has also brought blessing to those whose lives God has entrusted me with.

One of my neighbors frequently said, "Some people wait for life to bring them joy, while others bring joy to life!"

I desire to be the type of person who always shares joy, laughter, and optimism with others. Perhaps then they could know that joy is attainable for all! Joy is a gift. As we lean in toward the Giver, we allow our souls to be renewed and transformed into that which is beautiful, joy filled, and loving.

QUESTIONS TO PONDER

1. Looking at your life, which person or people have brought the greatest joy to your heart?

2. Do you wait for life to bring you joy, or do you bring it with you?

3. Do you find that some of the most joyful people are the most generous?

4

BEAUTY BLIND

August in America's heartland is breathtakingly beautiful, and it seemed especially so on the day my dad and I were headed off to retreat. Brilliant morning sunshine illuminated tufts of silk on row after row of sweet corn. We had our car windows rolled down to capture the clean, pure scent of rich soil and newly mowed grass, and our visors were flapped down to diffuse shimmers of light bouncing off passing lakes.

My father and I tried to make it our habit to travel the four and a half hours by car together. It was always a time for us to be alone without distractions or demands. It was also the perfect opportunity to unpack a year's worth of conversation before we embarked on a journey of silence during our retreat.

While we were unhurriedly cruising through the countryside, Dad began to tell me a little bit about the spiritual director who'd be leading that year's retreat. As soon as I heard the director's name, I recalled having heard about him before, actually a lot. According to Dad, this particular priest, Father Larry Gillick, was legendary.

I asked, "What makes him so wonderful?"

Dad responded, "Well, he's blind."

"Oh."

There was silence. Thoughts kept circling through my head, *How can this man handle the demands of priesthood with his disability? How on earth can he manage to connect with all of the men on the many retreats he directs each year?*

My annual trek with dad had always been an undeniable highlight every single year, but now having heard Father Gillick would be on retreat, I was even more certain we'd be inspired and challenged in our spiritual journeys and that our lives would never be the same.

There was a long, curving approach to the retreat house, sheltered on both sides with ancient trees and flowering shrubs. As we came around the last curve, an expansive lawn opened up and stretched as far as we could see, disappearing into Lake Elmo on the other side of the main retreat center. As often as I've pulled our car up into the lot, the sheer beauty of the place has moved me.

Attention had been given to the tiniest landscaping detail, and I'd always had a sense of the love and time that had been poured into creating such a gorgeous tribute to the Creator himself. A giant of a man we called "Big Mike" had tenderly maintained the grounds for decades. He had the physique of a middle linebacker for the Green Bay Packers, but he had the affectionate, gentle thumb of a master gardener. As a matter of fact, Big Mike went out of his way to be the very first person to greet each of the seventy men who arrived for retreat forty-seven weekends per year.

It was customary for men to be assigned to the same room year after year. It was a homecoming of sorts. Five generations of men in my family had occupied rooms in Manressa, a Dutch colonial-style house only a short distance from the main facility.

We were given some time to settle in and unpack in our rooms. For most of us, it wasn't shirts, socks, and pants that we were unpacking and stowing away. Instead we were setting aside fears, distractions, and stresses of work and home. We'd also been encouraged to leave behind phones, watches, and screens and lean into a simpler, quieter life.

Bells tolled to invite us to the physical chapel on the grounds, where we'd have our group gatherings. Those bells also invited us to the spiritual chapel of honesty, vulnerability, transparency, and, for many of us, healing. There were men present from every walk of life, every kind of personality, shape, and size, yet I could tell that we were also very much the same. We were each seeking our God through a journey of silence.

The chapel was the space where we men would gather at set times throughout the weekend, and what a space it was! Three walls were comprised of floor-to-ceiling glass panels that offered a panoramic view of Big Mike's immaculately groomed lawns and flower gardens to the lake beyond. Because local Minnesota birds and critters had been made to feel as welcome as we were, we could see wildlife up close and personal like never before. It was truly magnificent.

Captivated as I was by the beauty all around me, I didn't hear his footsteps at first. Actually I felt more than heard Father Gillick's arrival from the back of the chapel. Without aid of walking cane or human guide, our retreat master confidently walked to the very front of the chapel without speaking a single word. As he turned to face us, I knew we had officially begun.

Into this peace-filled silence, Father spoke, "We are not loved because we are good. We are good because we are loved."

Whoa. It seemed like such a simple sentence, but actually there was so much to assimilate that I couldn't get my mind wrapped around it right away. Later on, walking through the grounds and thinking deeply of its meaning, I could begin to grasp what Father Gillick was helping me to understand. It was our tendency to seek approval from others. We seemed to measure all the things we were doing before we measured who we were. The journey of silence was more about who we were becoming. We were unfinished works of art in the hands of the Artist. Silence invited us to be patient with the Master and ourselves.

I remember the day my dear friend Dawn asked me to have

some coffee with her. We'd already known each other for about six years, but she had been living and working in Germany at the time. It had been too long since we'd had a chance to catch up so I readily agreed. Then it hit me! I should invite her to jump in with our young adult group heading out to the Black Hills for a music festival. Dawn was immersed in the music scene in Germany, and we really needed a vocalist. Our worship band had been asked to open the festival, and thinking she'd enjoy the diversion, I invited her along. Of course she said yes.

There we were, sitting on our acre of blankets near the stage, having a catch-up session on life, music, and Germany when something the artist on stage was saying diverted our attention. He was talking about a "longing for true love, a love that doesn't disappoint."

With tears in her eyes, Dawn looked at me and said, "I've never felt true love."

Now I knew that Dawn deeply loved her family, and I had personally witnessed her family telling Dawn how very much they loved her. I didn't understand. What she said literally stopped my heart, like a car slamming on the brakes to avoid hitting a pedestrian. I thought to myself, *How can someone with so much beauty and tenderness make a statement like that?*

Dawn was homecoming queen selected by her classmates. She achieved academic success and was a very gifted, talented young woman. Yet her statement, "I've never felt true love," wrecked my heart. Overcome, I told her I would be right back and headed to a picnic table outside the park entrance. I just couldn't hold it back any longer and began to weep. I pondered, *How could she not know?*

In that moment, I was allowed to feel the deep desolation of her soul, her sense of abandonment, and her sense of emptiness. I realized too that those spaces were God-shaped holes only He could fill.

I walked back to our group on the blankets, still feeling a bit overwhelmed but comforted by the words Father Larry Gillick shared on retreat, "We are not loved because we are good. We are good because we are loved." It is not what we do, but who we are.

Our conversation together that day shaped our friendship into one that is, to this day, deep and everlasting. It was the day that both Dawn and I knew with certainty that we were loved—and would be loved—simply because of whose children we are. Dawn could see that the holes she felt in her heart came from thinking that she'd never be good enough. The insecurities she had came from comparing herself to other people, but she was already good enough. Through grace, each of us had a whole new perspective. We saw each other in a beautiful new light too.

Beauty for Father Larry Gillick is blind. If sight were relegated the use of eyes, he wouldn't be able to tell the difference between a rose and a dandelion or between Marilyn Monroe and Mother Theresa. I believe that Father Larry's blindness isn't a disability at all because he sees the true essence of a person. He's not trapped by cosmetic beauty, accomplishments or trends.

Is it possible that, more often than not, we are the ones who are blind? Is it possible that we are blind to our own uniqueness? Perhaps we are blind to being valued, being loved, or having significance and worth.

We would be wise to pay closer attention to the voices of hope, encouragement, inspiration, and love in our lives. We'd be especially wise to place ourselves in the chapel of honesty and enjoy a panoramic view of beauty and all its wonder.

Our lives are much like the beautiful grounds of the retreat center. Patience and silence will be required of us in order to see our own blindness. Then and only then will we arrive at a healthy awareness of our uniqueness and the beauty of those we are surrounded by. We too have beauty blind in all of us, waiting to be unearthed, discovered, and loved. Maybe, just maybe, Father Larry's blindness was the greatest gift to us that weekend. We are not loved because we are good. We are good because we are loved.

QUESTIONS TO PONDER

1. How do you see yourself in this statement, "We are not loved because we are good. We are good because we are loved"?

2. What do you see as your deepest blindness in life?

3. Have you totally misjudged someone due to your own blindness and then felt true remorse? Did you seek reconciliation?

5

"LET'S ROLL"

There was really no doubt about it. I'd gone completely crazy. I was climbing on board a chartered bus with forty or so giggling, energized middle schoolers, somewhat more mature high school students, and their soon-to-be-canonized chaperones. That trip had been in the planning phase for ages, and each time the team got together, it seemed like some new activity was added to our itinerary.

The thing is that I was climbing on board with a whole lot of people who had barely ventured beyond their own small, rural community. The shopping mall one hour away was big-time excitement. Only I had some idea of what was ahead of us, having been to our destination before. Only I truly felt the weight of having so many souls dependent upon me, their fearless leader.

Swallowing down my rising breakfast, I lugged my guitar and bags up our bus steps. As soon as I looked at the face of our bus driver though, I seriously laughed out loud. If this were our chaperone, all was going to be right with the world. The guy, Rich, looked like Hoss Cartwright from the old show *Bonanza*, if you can remember back that far.

For those of you who can't, Rich was a good ol' boy who wore a ten-gallon brown leather cowboy hat and an enormous grin to match. He was kind of leaning back in the bus seat with his feat propped up and looked like he didn't have a care in the world. The boisterous squeaks and shouts of adolescents didn't even seem to faze him much. (Nor did the staggering amounts of junk food that would soon wind up on the floor of his immaculate charter bus.)

More than anything else, Rich was a gentle giant who quickly became the head of our posse, and each of us grew to admire and respect him. He was papa bear, counselor, confidant, nurse's aid, and friend to all.

We had plans to make it to Pike's Peak in Cascade, Colorado, on our first day. Before we even got there, the drama started. Roughly thirty minutes before reaching Cascade and just barely passing into the Colorado Springs city limits, some of the students got elevation sickness and started dropping like flies. I thought, *Whoa! What's happening?*

Thankfully, our brave bus driver could calm the shrieking conscious kids and tend to the fallen ones. Rich knew quite a lot about altitude-related illnesses and quickly remedied the situation so we could be on our way.

Before long, we were pulling up to our hotel with majestic Pike's Peak as the backdrop. I could see on everyone's faces how amazed they were. Keep in mind: my crew hailed from an area that was flat for miles and miles and known for the massive turbines that captured winds whipping across the level prairie. The sight of America's Rocky Mountains held them spellbound.

Maybe it was because of the elevation sickness, but there was also a certain amount of anxiety and fear in our group. We were in completely foreign terrain. Some even told me they felt like they were "walking on the moon."

Underneath all of that, I think there was a bit of concern about the unknown. Our planning team communicated to the students and their parents all of the big details, but left out a bunch of the smaller ones, including a daily schedule.

In more than thirty years of ministry, I've learned there's

a whole lot of benefit in maintaining an element of suspense. Suspense creates teachable moments of trust. Trust is forged when we relinquish control, believe that everything works together for good, and we simply enjoy moments of wonder and awe.

Our entire trip to Colorado was built around a spectacular student conference that takes place in Colorado Springs each year. More than 3,500 young people from all states, denominations, and even many countries come to worship together in way that is simply life changing. I had attended in previous years and was so excited to allow the kids in our community to experience that same vibrant atmosphere.

In addition to the student conference, we visited Garden of the Gods, the "top geological wonder in Colorado."[2] The red rock formations date back millions of years and have been spiritual sites for Native Americans throughout more recent centuries. We planned praise and worship and an outdoor mass at one of the summits. That evening remains one of the most profound and unforgettable nights of my life!

A really gigantic item on our itinerary caused not just one night of lost sleep. I woke up one morning thinking, *Why am I so anxious? Why do I feel so restless?* Then I pondered some more, *Oh, yeah. White-water rafting.*

I had invited all of the students and chaperones to jump into the unknown. I had never been rafting in my life ... in any boat on any body of water. But I was somehow supposed to be a knowledgeable, fearless leader! Right.

Rich looked at me across the hotel breakfast table with his big, smirky smile and asked, "Hey, are you ready, Captain?"

I thought, *Captain? Who awarded me that title? Maybe Chief Bottle Washer, but certainly not Captain!* I didn't dare reveal to anyone just how apprehensive I was, but it seemed Rich could

---

[2] http://www.pikes-peak.com/about-garden-of-the-gods

already tell. In his quiet, reassuring way, he reminded me that everyone was going to follow my lead, so he laughed.

"Put your smile back on, like a saddle on a horse, and let's roll!"

Our bus rolled to a stop in Buena Vista, Spanish for "beautiful view," one of the premiere white-water rafting destinations in the world. This pristine Colorado mountain town is located along the Arkansas River, a major tributary of the mighty Mississippi. Buena Vista sits 8,000 feet above sea level and is eclipsed by 14,000-foot mountains. Wow! Every summer, enthusiasts converge on the town to seek thrills on the wild and mild rapids of the Arkansas River.

We were all corralled on our designated spot near the outfitter when a gangly, rugged, good-looking rafting guide greeted us. He had a silly smile that instantly put everyone at ease. I was sure he had a lot of experience with newcomers and their nerves.

"Welcome!" Jason said. "We're so glad you're here! You are about to embark on an adventure that you'll remember for the rest of your life. So let's get you registered and suited up."

Too late to turn back or wuss out now! It's time to journey into the unknown! This was the little pep talk I was giving myself because Rich had to remind me yet again that everyone was following my lead.

We were fitted with wetsuits that felt more like a straitjackets, life vests, and some special shoes. Let's just say it wasn't the most becoming outfit I've worn in my life, but safety comes way before beauty.

Once more, we were all standing around in a loose circle, and Jason commenced to go over his checklist. It sounded a lot like something you might hear from flight attendant preparing for takeoff. You know you need to listen, but you kind of don't want to because of all the worst-case scenarios you'll be reminded of. All I could think of was, *Oh my goodness. This is it. Life as I know it. Over.*

My wandering brain was pulled back into sharp focus when I heard Jason say, "And another thing: If by chance you fall out of the raft, make sure you keep your feet pointing upstream. If they're pointing downstream, your legs could get caught under rocks. They could break pretty bad and/or trap you in the rapids."

Gulp.

"Lastly, the state of Colorado requires us to tell all of you who are rafting that there is always the possibility of death."

There was total silence. Everyone was looking at me, the so-called "Captain (not) America," the "(not-so-much) Leader."

I'm thinking, *What have I just done? I have willingly put forty souls in harm's way. I am totally responsible for their well-being! Should we stay, or do we go?* It was such a relief that no one could hear what was rattling around in my brain during that defining moment.

Several of the seventh-grade girls were having a slumber party in the circle and were oblivious to the last two instructions. Other kids looked at me with sad, puppy dog eyes, as if their favorite toy were just ripped away. And naturally there were those who were even more stoked after hearing Jason's ominous speech and couldn't wait to get their paddles in the river.

Now there was a pause. Feeling the gravity of everyone's stares, I looked at Jason and shouted, "Let's roll!"

Instantly there were cheers and a mad scramble for the rafts. We were all divided up among the seven rafts and seven guides. One by one, the rafts departed. I waved at each of the teams heading downstream, noting the nervous smiles on their faces.

"Have fun! I'll be praying for you!"

I thought, *As if that gives them any kind of solace.*

Then Jason looked at me. "Are you ready?"

"Let's roll!" With the hesitation of someone who had just been invited to jump out of a plane at fifteen thousand feet, I yelled, "Whoo-hoo!"

Jason directed me to take a seat in the back to oversee operations. (I think he actually felt that, at the least, I'd be good ballast. At the best, I'd be out of his way.)

Four of our sons—Josh, Jonny, Zach, and Nathan—were also

assigned to my boat. As we put in, the current moved nice and gently, and we were like, "Oh, this isn't bad at all!"

Oops! Before we knew it, the waters went from class two (rough water) to class three (some rocks but no big danger), and we began to take on some water. Jason shouted instructions to help us maneuver around boulders rising above the rapids.

Thanks to massive spring runoff, we suddenly found ourselves in class four waters (exceptional rafting experience needed). These waters could immerse you into oblivion and crunch your broken body into the rocks.

I'm telling you that it was a rite of passage for my posse and me. As a group, we learned a lot that day. We realized that we would have never experienced the beauty of the Arkansas River and all its breathtaking scenery, had we allowed fear, anxiety, and uncertainty to set up camp in our hearts.

Those rapids favored no one. They tossed us around relentlessly, like sailboats in a hurricane. Just when we were moving from fear into exhilaration, we rounded a bend in the river, and the waters calmed back into ones and more ones.

"Yes! Whoo-hoo! We made it!"

We were exhausted and sopping wet but basking in the glow of achievement. After two and a half hours of wrestling the water, we made it! And every last one of us shared an unbreakable bond that only adversity and uncertainty could produce.

What a ride. What a *ride*!

From the moment our bus pulled out of the church parking lot and to the moment it pulled back in, our group experienced an adventure and beauty that we would have otherwise never known. We were allowed a satisfaction of accomplishment and faced such adversities that we would never have conquered if we had allowed fear and anxiety to enslave us.

What holds you back from an adventure? What kind of breathtaking view do you long to see from your raft? What would you do if you weren't afraid?

QUESTIONS TO PONDER

1. What is one fear that has held you back from what might have been an exhilarating experience?

2. Sometimes your decision hanging in the balance will impact others. Will you lead by example and lean into life or retreat from it to a life that is safe and secure?

3. Who has pushed you beyond yourself? How?

6

INNOCENCE REDISCOVERED

I'd like to introduce you to Ruby and Dorothy, two amazing South Dakota sisters. Ruby was born in the year 1903; Dorothy was born in 1904. Though they were born in Minnesota and attended school in Saskatchewan, Canada, they spent most of their years east of the Missouri River in South Dakota. The two sisters shared a home, a bountiful garden, and the respect of neighbors and peers until each died at the exceptional age of 108 years old.

What a gift for Ruby and Dorothy to journey through life with a sister who was also her very best friend! One can only imagine how they marveled together at the invention of automobiles, rockets, submarines, and airplanes. As professional businesswomen, Ruby and Dorothy witnessed the evolution of heavy typewriters to computers, the internet, and Skype. Scientists even landed on the moon and explored outer space during their lifetimes.

Through my in-laws, who were neighbors and good friends of Ruby and Dorothy, I learned that these two sisters loved to share the story about their 1950s family trip to Disneyland in Anaheim, California. It seems fitting then that my life intersected with theirs via Walt Disney and the sisters' extraordinary expression of generosity.

Around the time of Thanksgiving one year, a piece of mail arrived in our box addressed to my wife. It wasn't an ordinary letter. It looked like a party on paper! As soon as Dawn walked in through our kitchen door, the kids and I stampeded her and practically tore the envelope open for her while she held it.

Our crazy excitement was well worth it when we saw the stunned look on Dawn's face. We had just received an invitation to the trip of our dreams. All nineteen members of the "Jim & Bonnie" family were traveling together to Walt Disney World with all expenses paid through a specific gift from Ruby and Dorothy.

Now I have to say right here that Jim and Bonnie are definitely people who freely give everything they are and have. They take care of people simply because they love them. That's it. When the sisters' attorney first told them about this travel gift, Jim and Bonnie tried to give it back. They explained they couldn't accept it. All they wanted to do was be good neighbors and loyal friends. Apparently it doesn't work like that, so Jim and Bonnie paid it forward in a selfless way and gathered the whole family together.

Now I was in disbelief about the invitation and said to Dawn, "You've got to be kidding!"

"No way!" she burst out. "Mom and Dad are making all the arrangements! We all get to go this January!"

Anyone involved in student ministry—or ministry of any kind—knows what a huge deal this is. Vacation is one rare thing. Paid vacation is certainly a different thing altogether.

Added to the thrill of being able to spend quality time with grandparents, parents, and children all in the same place at the same time was the fact that most of my five sons had never been on an airplane before. The whipped cream, chocolate sauce, and Maraschino cherry on the cake was getting to be at Walt Disney World together.

I kept thinking, *This will be a blast for the kids!* I didn't really give much thought to my fifty-year-old self. I figured we eight older folks would be hard-pressed to find something to do for seven days at an amusement park. Really!

On the appointed, eagerly awaited day, we left behind our parkas, mittens, and snow boots and trucked off to the airport. My wife and I felt like kids ourselves while watching our boys' amazed faces.

Our sons experienced a lot of firsts that trip, like boarding an actual airplane, experiencing the thrust of the plane's engines lifting into the atmosphere, and seeing their world 33,000 feet below their seats. As far as I was concerned, the real magic was already happening. We were leaving subzero temps and a foot of snow in exchange for blue skies and palm trees.

With our seats and tray tables in the upright and locked position, we touched down at Orlando Airport. As the engine's reverse thrust slowed our aircraft, I could see exhilaration and relief on our boys' faces.

"We're here! We made it!"

I couldn't help thinking that our family seemed to be bubbling over in the same goofy, squirrelly way as Moe, Larry, and Curly in The Three Stooges!

We were the last the group to arrive at our Disney resort, and I can't even describe the pandemonium that ensued. Every last one of us knew how very special it was to be together in this way, and we couldn't wait to let the games begin.

The next thing we know, the rooms and luggage had been quickly sorted, and all nineteen of us were shuttling off to the theme parks. We were squished into our transport like sardines and were delirious with fatigue, but the kids in our group couldn't wait to get to get on some rides. I smiled for them as a courtesy, but I would have leapt at the chance to sit in the resort hot tub with an adult beverage or two.

Once we all formulated a game plan and funneled through the Magic Kingdom admission gates, it turned into stampede toward ride lines. I thought, *This is crazy!* I couldn't keep up with the leaping, skipping frenzy. In the midst of the chaos, I felt a tiny hand placed into mine and heard my name.

"Uncle Dave, let's go to It's a Small World." The voice belonged to my little three-year-old niece, Elizabeth. If any one word could describe Elizabeth, it would be "darling." I now know why God gave Dawn and me five boys. I would have spoiled this one so much that it would have broken the bank.

There I was, tucked into a boat with little Elizabeth, maneuvering along in the water while costumed dolls popped out and sang to us. She was bouncing up and down, singing along while her face glowed with joy. It seemed impossible that she could keep up that level of excitement all day. I was wrong.

It was only later in the day already full of adventures that she looked up at me and asked, "Uncle Dave, can I sit up on your shoulders?"

I had apparently been promoted from "traveling buddy" to "Über driver." Chances are, I was far more exhausted than she could ever be, but how could I disappoint my young companion? Besides, my brother- and sister-in-law had entrusted her care to me. I quickly agreed and hoisted up Elizabeth.

It didn't occur to me until later that I had been entrusted to Elizabeth's care. She was the one leading the journey on and between amusement park rides. Elizabeth's energy and enthusiasm sustained us as we galloped our way around the Magic Kingdom. Through Elizabeth's three-year-old eyes, I was challenged to see the world. Through her, I could see the world was truly, indescribably magnificent.

That first day started a bit of a trend. Elizabeth paired herself up with me every day after that, and like a mini general, she briefed me each morning on what her plans were. I was the guardian, but that paled in significance to the job she gave herself, GPS. (Surprisingly that didn't stand for "General Pint Size.")

Elizabeth strategically mapped out all of the places she wanted to go and knew precisely how to get there. At times I thought we were lost, but she would reassure me that she knew exactly where we were. And she was right!

Through each day's excursions, I had a little three-year-old girl inviting me to her table of trust. Really, it was not just a table. It was a banquet filled with delicacies like wonder, amazement, and surprise. Somewhere along the line, I had forgotten what those unique seasonings were. I was more familiar with the blander flavors of responsibility, duty, and commitment.

As an adult, I had abandoned what I considered to be childlike ways. On that wonderful vacation to Florida with my family, I heard a little voice echoing through the chambers of my heart, calling me back to the innocence of discovery. It was a voice of deep, abiding joy that beckoned me to really smile again. It was a voice of trust that reminded me, "Each day is a gift. You need to really live it!" It was a voice of love that invited me to once again become vulnerable and embrace an unknown journey. It was a voice of hope, a confidence that I would allow myself to continue to taste life's zest once again in the days ahead.

We still swap stories and memories of our week together with the whole clan in Florida. We marvel at what a huge blessing it was to spend uninterrupted time getting to really know one another again. We owe a great debt of gratitude to Ruby, Dorothy, Jim, and Bonnie for reminding us that nothing matters more than faith and family.

Among the many lessons taught to us through the selflessness of two wonderful South Dakota sisters, one stands out to me especially. It is not the duration of life that matters; it is the quality of life.

Ruby and Dorothy maintained a disposition of the heart day after day for 108 years. Certainly their lives were not absent of challenges, difficulties, and sadness. Their attitude toward them made all the difference. They held within them a certain innocence and appreciation for all of life's blessings that kept them oriented to true north. They savored the myriad of unfamiliar flavors served up to them each new year. And no matter the path or circumstance, their internal GPS allowed them to know where they'd come from, where they were going, and how they were going to get there ... like Elizabeth.

QUESTIONS TO PONDER

1. Have you sought a childlike wonder, imagination, and impulse to color outside the lines of creativity?

2. I've seen young people who have hearts of seventy-year olds and seventy-year olds who have hearts of those in their twenties. Growing old is a disposition of the heart. It's either living a life of resignation or living a life with all its possibilities. Where do you see yourself on a pendulum of life: resigned ... existing ... living?

7

TRANSMISSIONS

From time to time, I find myself engaged in deep, philosophical discussions in the most unlikely of places. After a workout at the gym, an older gentleman said to me, "I will tell you what you value by what you fear."

I thought to myself, *That is really an odd statement!* It struck a chord in me though. After mulling it over for a while, I admitted I definitely had fears. We all do ... and more than one, if we're being honest about it. What seemed apparent was that most people have a fear of death. Surprisingly that isn't a fear I can personally claim. I fear something else, suffering.

For as long as I can remember, I've never liked suffering. As matter of fact, at the age of eight or so, my father invited me to join him and my five siblings on an excursion to the family farm. Sadly it was to bury our beloved Labrador, King. I declined. I couldn't imagine having to say goodbye to a friend I dearly loved. It burdened me that King might have been in pain before he passed. It also hurt that I could never again bury my face in his black fur and share all my secrets. Death seemed so cruel, unfair, and permanent.

So after the discussion at the gym, I realized the man was absolutely correct. I feared suffering, so it followed that what I truly value in life is joy in life itself. Life is to be lived! How can we go through life and not happily savor its flavors?

From my earliest years, I have always found great joy in life. My mother frequently reminded me that I was the happiest baby of her six. Apparently I was content and smiling from the cradle onward. Maybe that's why I am attracted to those who truly embrace life, to those who have such a joyful spirit that they treat each person they meet as if he or she were the most adored person in the world. I know a guy like that. I've also been blessed to call him friend for more than thirty years.

The very day I met Sid, I knew it wouldn't be the last time I'd see him. Sid was bursting with optimism, so much so that I thought, *Sooner or later, he's going to have to come down from his heavenly place! Sooner or later, reality will settle in, Sid's wings will be clipped, and he'll plunge back to reality.*

Believe it or not, Sid still has wings. He may have arrived back to earth, but his love for life and his optimism are absolutely contagious. In his simple way, Sid unlocked a treasure for me. I learned that what I choose to pursue is what I will become. When I, like Sid, look for good in others, I'll become good. When I am kind to others, kindness envelops me. Joy is found.

Sid, his girlfriend Linda, and I ended up attending the same university together. One day, we decided to go on a road trip not too far off campus. We had a plan to spend an entire day hanging out at a neighboring city's mall. We didn't have any kind of shopping list, let alone money, so we didn't have plans to buy a single thing. It was more about us three just hanging out together and people-watching. We simply found it entertaining to see all sorts of people running around buying things, as if this or that was going to satisfy their hearts' longings. In the end, the only longing the three of us had was to get the heck out of there after watching hours of shopping obsession.

Our trek back to the university was an adventure in itself, clunking down the interstate in Sid's makeshift car. Linda sat in the front seat, squashed between Sid and me. We passed the time swapping hilarious stories of our experiences so far at school, with each story more getting ridiculous than the last.

With his exuberant storytelling and crazy antics, Sid cranked our laughter to the point where we were doubled over and gasping for air. Desperate, Linda swung up her arms in surrender because she couldn't take it anymore. Apparently neither could Sid's car! As Linda lifted up her arms, she accidentally knocked the gearshift, vaulting Sid's car into reverse going sixty-five miles an hour! The engine completely croaked, which was even funnier to us than anything so far.

I was starting to think I should be checking the car seats for suspicious wetness when the car came to a rolling stop at the side of the road. More convulsive laughter erupted when the car finally stopped moving.

We were so amazed that we were all still alive that of course we laughed again. We laughed hard enough that I think Linda probably wet her pants. Sid, on the other hand, was gasping for breath in utter disbelief about what had just happened. He wasn't mad or frustrated. He was as immersed in laughter as Linda and me. (As for me, I was laughing only because it wasn't my car! Obviously I didn't tell them that!)

We slowly calmed ourselves in the car on the side of the highway. It became utterly quiet. The obnoxiously loud engine was no longer running. I was pretty sure the transmission was shot and the engine couldn't possibly turn over. But imagine our shock when Sid turned the key in the ignition and the car's engine fired up! The relief on Linda's face affirmed that their relationship was going to be kicked into gear along with the engine. We made it safely back to our dorms and swore it would be a good long time before we went people-watching at the mall again.

What I realized that day is that life sometimes throws us in reverse when we least expect it. For Sid, it was when his father died of a heart attack just when Sid was graduating from high school. How does one recover from that? What is it like to have to become the man of the household at an age when you're just discovering who you are as a man?

Sid handled all of that and more. That is just one of the things that has been so amazing about him. In the thirty years I've known Sid, he continues to exude joy, life, and optimism, regardless of difficulty or circumstance.

There is so much to be learned in this journey we call life. There's also much to reflect upon in Sid's response to the unexpected. We all react, but how we respond makes all the difference in this world. You see, Sid's joy makes all the difference to a whole lot of people. It's a decision he makes every day and every week of his life. Don't get me wrong. I'm sure that Linda, Sid's wife of thirty years, could fill in the rest of the narrative that I've left out. But I have to believe that much of what she'd share would echo what I've written.

Friendships like Sid's and mine only come once in a lifetime. And what a lifetime it has been! We have laughed, we've tasted loss, we've reflected together while on retreat, and we've struggled, married, sent children off to college, and embraced this journey we call life.

If life were measured in a cup, Sid's would be overflowing. It would be full and overflowing with the things that matter, qualities that cannot be purchased at a store. It would be full of the joy Sid has chosen each and every day of his life, an existence in which he has chosen to rise above even when life's challenges threw him in reverse at sixty-five miles an hour.

QUESTIONS TO PONDER

1. What events have thrown your life in reverse, and how did you respond?

2. How do you see the cup, half full or half empty?

3. Who is the person most full of optimism in your life?

8

ENDGAME

My first year of college, I was feeling a bit overwhelmed, just like any incoming freshman. And just like any freshman, I was dealing with the big questions: Who am I going to become in the middle of this pool of humanity? What significant impact can I make on the world? What gifts and talents do I have that will make any kind of difference? And just as in any collegiate atmosphere, there are always those pleasant distractions that lure us away from academia. I know what you're thinking: girls, bars, and so on. You might be surprised.

I was sitting in our collegiate chapel when an older gentleman strolled in wearing a full-length black robe complete with hood, scapular that draped across his chest to the floor, cowl sleeves, and a beautiful silver cross. Instantly I recognized him as a Benedictine monk. With a huge, endearing smile, he introduced himself to me.

"Hello! I'm Brother Placid, and this is my dog Hoover." Leaning closer, he added, "Spelled like the vacuum cleaner."

Hoover was a 130-pound bullmastiff that quickly became the mascot and built-in, four-legged security detail of my future home, our student center.

Brother Placid exclaimed, "Welcome to the Newman Center!"

Taken a little aback by his friendliness, I said, "Thanks. What is this place? I gather we meet up on Sundays for church, but are there other events that happen here during the week?"

He replied, "Well, for starters, how about a game of ping-pong? Right now?"

At that point, Brother Placid struck a chord in me. I loved that game. I've always enjoyed being competitive. At the same time, I felt awful that I would take this little Benedictine brother to the cleaners in the best of three rounds.

Humility was the first virtue I learned at the student center. I lost all three games. Brother Placid was practically dancing around on the other side of the table, relishing in his easy victory.

In truth, a greater victory had been won that day. That day, Brother captured my heart with his warm smile and welcoming spirit. Brother Placid and his dog Hoover transformed the atmosphere of the student center with their boundless enthusiasm. Brother's simple invitation to journey toward hope made all the difference. No, he didn't have all the answers to life's questions. But the way he responded to life's challenges spoke volumes to those around him.

Brother Placid always had a way of making everyone feel welcomed. He was the doorway to hospitality and love. I marveled at his life of love and simplicity. He never preached at us; nor did he give any theological dissertation on the spiritual life. What Brother did was emulate a servant, one who greeted us each day with a smile. He deposited a faith, which spurred us beyond our silly self-interests and sprinkled hope along with his smile, reminding us all that each day was a gift meant to be treasured.

Brother Placid would bite at each opportunity to engage in meaningful conversations. It didn't matter or where or when. He made himself available to anyone needing to just talk it out. He also had the gift of making us feel like we were more important than anything else going on and focused completely on us while he listened without judgment to what we had on our hearts. Simply said, he gave all of us one of the greatest gifts he had, his time.

And then there was Hoover. If you're not familiar with the breed, you should Google a bullmastiff picture, and you'll know in an instant what I mean when I say. The dog was huge. He had a goofy, slobbery grin, and in spite of his massive size, he was generally obedient to his master, except of course when it came to the love of his life, Sabrina.

Sabrina, in the sweetest way possible, resembled a true Southern belle. She was charming and well spoken with the slightest Southern drawl, and she could accessorize like nobody's business. Sabrina was probably appalled that we guys liked to lounge around in ratty T-shirts and gym shorts, while she liked to wear perfectly coordinated outfits that matched her hair and makeup. Hoover was convinced that Sabrina was his biggest dream come to life on two legs, and he just couldn't seem to leave her alone.

I swear, every single time Sabrina would come to the student center, Hoover would meet her before she even got to the door and chase her all around. Seriously, the two were running down halls, around corners, and through doors. It was totally hilarious to the rest of us! Sabrina would be shrieking, Hoover would be barking, and Brother Placid would be trying to keep up with the two of them shouting, "Hoover! Hoover! Stop!" Brother would blush profusely and stammer at Sabrina about how totally sorry he was and how totally embarrassed he was. We guys would laugh our faces off, joking that Brother Placid was trying to make Hoover adopt the same vow of chastity that he took, but the dog was a total renegade.

As I look back at this treasured time at the student center, I have come to realize more than ever before that what Brother Placid did and who he was that had the most significant impact.

These many, many years later—and even while Brother Placid is no longer among us on earth—his legacy of warm hospitality continues through those of us who were blessed to learn from his example. Brother Placid's endgame was love.

What will your legacy be?

QUESTIONS TO PONDER

1. Who is your Brother Placid? Who is the one who has always made you feel welcome?

2. Name a person (or people) whose faith is simple and yet profound, strongly impacting your life.

3. Is love the motivation of your heart? Does love fuel what you do?

9

SNOW AND LIGHT

It's Christmas Eve, and I am ambling down the streets of our quaint, historic town, Cedarburg, Wisconsin. Fat, wet snowflakes have arrived this evening, as if to welcome each visitor into a mystery of waiting and childlike expectation of what is to come. A horse-drawn carriage bedecked with jingling bells, lights, and garland transports holiday sojourners across our snow-covered downtown. Festive decorations shimmer in the eyes of the young, the old, and their four-legged friends wagging along beside them. Each storefront along Main Street proclaims the season with artfully constructed displays to entice and delight us. It's a Christmas Eve painting come to life.

As unimaginably beautiful as this night is, something far greater, longing, is underpinning the entire scene. It can't be seen with the naked eye, but it's there nonetheless. I can sense that every heart longs to somehow capture all of the beauty and hold it close—to draw it inward, shape it, and release it again in its own creative way.

This Christmas season, I am reflecting especially on creative longing and the mystery of motherhood. In the hustle and busyness of Christmas, it's easy to lose sight of the peace-filled wonder of the manger: the brand-new mama, Mary, cuddling her precious

49

newborn baby, Jesus, and Joseph protecting both of them in the shelter of his arms, speechless with awe.

Mothers, especially expectant mothers, must be so keenly aware of the creative process. A mother is privileged to hold inside her another heart beating in harmony with hers. She experiences the flutters and movements of her child and marvels that she'll one day hold her new baby in her arms. The created life wrapped within mystery and within her reflects the awesomeness of his Creator.

Two moms are foremost in my mind as I stroll along in the winter wonderland: my wife Dawn and my mother Constance. Both women have been infused with amazing gifts and talents. It's seems like they've always had some craft-type project in the works: chalk portraits, hand-sewn mittens, painted birdhouses, or needlework. Both share a passion for music, dance, song, and art in general. Lucky for my five sons and me, Dawn and Mom also charm us with creative, home-cooked meals that satisfy our appetites for family and food. Still, with all of those wonderful gifts, there's some kind of longing within them and me for the beautiful and for that which is unknown.

In our childhood, my brother Paul and I would sneak into the living room to the small pile of gifts carefully arranged beneath our family Christmas tree. Somehow our mom always managed to catch us in the act of peeking, peeling, or shaking to figure out what was hidden behind the wrapping paper and tape. To this very day, I admit I have an almost insatiable desire to pursue the mystery of what is hidden or waiting for me.

My wife has figured out a smooth way to keep me from leading our sons into my former Christmas-peeking habits. Every gift under the tree has a nice little tag on it, but there's some kind of fake name. Each name represents one of the five boys or me, the biggest kid. Part of the hilarity is figuring out which one of us is "Wumperdinkle" or "Franktaculous." Even if one of us manages to get a package in our grubby little mitts, there's no way to guess who is receiving what. I'm always amazed that we can actually make it to Christmas Eve without opening the presents and that we actually enjoy the mystery of the unknown.

Sometimes the gift isn't what we hold in our hands. It's what we hold within our hearts. The special something within us, once unwrapped, reveals our own uniqueness and beauty. Some people choose to put that special something on display, much like Cedarburg's quaint little storefronts boasting bright tinsel and flashing lights.

Others' gifts shine particularly bright through meekness and humility. It isn't tinsel or light that draws attention. It's quiet simplicity. It seems that those who possess this special something have a deep reserve of generosity and choose to pour richly into the lives they've been entrusted with. They pour their time, loyalty, and devotion.

Such has been my experience with Dawn and Mom. These two mothers uniquely possess gifts of unselfishness, encouragement, patience, and love. They have, in turn, deposited these same traits into the hearts and lives of their children.

I truly believe that mothers are especially dear to the heart of God. They have accepted a vocation that has no trophies, blue ribbons, diplomas, or letters of recommendation. They don't wear shiny honor medallions pinned all over themselves like the baubles on their family Christmas trees, though their medallions would far exceed the baubles. These mothers treat each of their children as if he or she is a gift waiting to be opened in due time. With patience and trust, these moms help repair torn packaging and unstuck tape until the day arrives for their children to be the men and women God in His goodness created.

Let's be frank: Some kids have the added benefit of brighter wrappings and fancier bows. Moms who deeply love their children will see beyond any temporal things and know that the greater beauty lies within. Dreams, possibilities, and hopes are waiting to be discovered. Believing in each child's own, unique God-given beauty, she tucks them in at night, prayerfully entrusting them to their Creator.

I'll never forget the night that I had to say goodbye to my mother forever. On her last night in the hospital, Constance Ruth Kinsman was a true evergreen. Near to her bedside, like ornaments, stood all of us kids and my dad, her spouse for more than fifty-three years. You see, her contributions were the more precious ornaments through the example of her own life: fidelity, integrity, joy, humility, servanthood, meekness, and hope. What adorned our family even more than any of these beautiful things was love.

That final night with Mom, we witnessed a moment that will be forever etched in our hearts. Dad invited all of us children to take hold of each other's hands as we surrounded our mother's bed. Together we voiced prayers of affection for our mom, offered countless prayers of thanksgiving, and added many prayers that only could be formed with tears, not words.

While we were connected in this way, Mom took her last breath. Our father, her bridegroom, solemnly caressed Mom's face and lovingly placed kisses as if there were a special, endless reserve of them, set aside just for her.

Mom's death was sudden and unexpected. By the time I was able to travel the far-too-many miles to the hospital, she was unresponsive. It was such a stark contrast to the vibrant, energetic person she was on our visit home not too long before that.

My family and I lived out of state but made time to get back to see Mom and Dad as often as we could. When it was time for us to head back to our own home and our van was close to exploding with kids, luggage, toys, and dog, there was a little ritual. Mom and Dad would come outside to see us off. While we were practically hanging out of windows and doors, the two of them would go around to each of us and give us kisses, sometimes even to the more important action figure toys.

On the last visit home though, only my mother carried out

the ritual. She seemed to take extra time with each one of her grandsons and kissed them so very tenderly. Waving out the windows like we always did, I glanced up at the rearview mirror. Every other trip, my exhausted parents returned to the house and collapsed in their easy chairs. That day, Mom hadn't moved from her spot in the driveway. She continued to stand there, smile, and wave. It was as if, somewhere deep in her spirit, she knew her earthly time with us would be coming to a close.

In every season and in every celebration, let us set time away from the busyness to honor the women who have so generously poured themselves into the lives of others. The dreams, hopes, and passions of these mothers may not have come to full fruition in the course of their own lifetimes, but the light-filled legacy continues.

QUESTIONS TO PONDER

1. How has your mother or mother figure spoken life into you?

2. What gifts and talents has she or someone else encouraged you to dream, develop, and create?

3. If your mother or guardian were sitting with you now, what would you say to express from your heart the gratitude you have for her?

10

FOR BETTER OR
FOR WORSE?

It was an ideal Saturday morning in spring. Our bedroom windows were thrown wide open to catch the fragrance and sound of the nearby Missouri River. Added to the aromas of damp earth and lilac trees surrounding our courtyard was the mouth-watering smell of freshly baked bread. Early in our marriage, my wife and I began a weekend tradition where we'd let a loaf of frozen bread dough thaw and rise overnight Friday, and whoever was awake first on Saturday morning would put the loaf in the oven. There was nothing like waking up to my precious bride and enjoying a fresh cup of java with a slice of freshly baked bread smothered in butter! (I think I have the right order: bride, then java, and then bread with butter!)

On that Saturday, my precious wife was just a couple months pregnant with our first little one. The reason why I call her "precious" is because, while we were dating, I'd surprise Dawn with a Precious Moments figurine whenever I found one I thought she'd enjoy.

Dawn was petite and a little bit shy, and she had a look that was so endearing that it really resembled the figurines' faces.

When she'd react to something sentimental in a book, a movie, or possibly something I'd say, a tear would trickle down the side of her cheek, and I would be there to catch it. She was my own precious, flesh-and-blood doll.

Dawn was one of the unfortunate types of women who began her pregnancy feeling sick and never quite shook it off until the baby was born. It helped her to start each day out slowly, which was nice for me because we could lay around together on the days I didn't need to head to the office early.

While we were hanging around on that idyllic day, I mentioned to my bride that one of our dearest friends in life, Janine, had invited us out for lunch at the new Chinese restaurant in town. Janine also asked along a young man named Frank, who had just moved to town and was working with her in the attorney general's office.

It wasn't a surprise that Dawn declined. Chinese didn't seem to sit well with her on good days, and she was still pale and nauseated that morning after eating only soda crackers. Concerned she wasn't eating enough, I tried to coax her into letting me bring back something to eat later. In the end, she decided that fried rice actually sounded pretty good and gave me a kiss as I headed out the door.

I arrived at the Chinese restaurant, settled in with Janine and her new colleague, Frank, and tucked into a heaping plate of spicy General Tso's chicken. Let's just say that the meal had a whole lot more spice than the conversation that was taking place. Frank was a very kind and sincere man. He was clearly introverted though, and the awkward new-to-town conversation had more stops than starts. Thinking that maybe such a public setting was making him nervous, I invited him and Janine to come over to Dawn's and my apartment and have some chocolate cake and fresh coffee.

Janine answered for both of them, exclaiming, "Sure! But I'd like to take Frank over to my house to see the garden, and then we'll head over to your place."

With plans made, I drove home to tell Dawn and make preparations for their arrival. By this time, Dawn had some color in her cheeks and was excited to have company coming to visit. I set a little place at our table for her and poured the fried rice into a bowl. She dug right in with gusto and hummed along with the radio between big bites.

Since my wife was happy in her own little world, I got to work cutting cake and making a fresh pot of coffee. Thinking she was still at the table, I was chatting about lunch at the Chinese place and commenting about the music on the radio. When I finally turned to ask her about something, I noticed she wasn't there anymore. Our apartment was small enough to figure out that there was only one other place she could possibly be, the bathroom. We hadn't been married quite a year yet, so a closed door to the bathroom meant it was a bit of a no-fly zone. I hadn't yet interrupted her in that sacred space when the door was closed.

That day, I did. I cracked the door only wide enough to whisper, "Say, honey? When you're finished, I'm gonna need to use the bathroom."

There was no response. I guess the fried rice did not befriend her stomach. All I heard was a quiet moan. I'm thinking to myself, *Boy, I'm so glad she didn't have General Tso's chicken!*

Knowing that our guests would be arriving before too long, I meandered into the kitchen to tidy up. I washed a few dishes, wiped down the table, and filled the saltshaker. *Hmmmm*, I thought. *I wonder if she's okay.*

The door was still the way I left it, cracked open just a little bit. Once more, I stood outside the bathroom and asked if she was feeling all right. She made that awful sound women do when they're getting super-annoyed, the stuck-in-the-throat-growl noise. Sensing pending doom, I vacated the area, like any gentleman would.

I started fluffing the couch pillows and straightening the edges of my record collection.

Uh-oh. It was becoming obvious that Dawn's stomach wasn't the only one agitated. *This time*, I thought, *She better answer. And she better be done!*

I went back to the bathroom door, only this time I opened it just wide enough to see her face. I looked right into her eyes and said louder than before, but as politely as I could, "Honey, I really need to go the bathroom!"

What happened next was something I never dreamed I'd experience in my marriage to a real-life Precious Moments doll. Her heretofore suppressed, feisty Irish spirit came out with a vengeance.

Dawn shouted, "Just wait a second!"

I was shocked! It took me so much by surprise that I burst out laughing. Yes, laughing. My sweet, smiling bride had somehow turned into a monster. Tears were streaming down my face, and I was choking out great, gusty laughs when I realized Chinese food, laughing, and needing to go the bathroom are a lethal combination.

You won't believe what happened then. Dawn, somehow as shocked as I was at her crazy outburst, started laughing as hard as I was. We sounded like two hysterical hyenas at a feeding frenzy.

I yelled out, "Move!" proceeding to back toward her like some huge dump truck making a delivery.

Dawn saw that I was moving fast toward her, and her face froze with terror. There was no time for delay, and she flew off the toilet seat like a scud missile and landed with a thud only a few feet away from total disaster. All the while, she and I were still laughing uncontrollably!

I'm embarrassed to say that I exploded chemical warfare all over myself and the surrounding area. There were no survivors. Scant inches away from my feet was my half-clad wife wriggling to escape, convulsing with laughter and fear. I think I scarred her forever. I know for sure that we scarred our visitors forever. They couldn't have timed their arrival to our apartment for cake and coffee any better.

I know what you're thinking. *What did this guy just reveal to me? How could he have been so crude to share such a not-so-intimate moment?* Well, when laughter subtly begins to cease in your relationship, so does your zest for being in that relationship.

Just before the day I was to marry Dawn, my father said to me, "Dave, the best thing you can do for your children is to love your wife. Laugh with her, and love her."

After more than twenty-five years with my wife, I can now see he was wise and he was right. From the roots to the branches of our family tree, we have been graced with over two hundred years of fidelity. I am sure there are many stories among the marriages that would rival the challenges we seemed to face. Those tales would contain the trials and hardships of the Great Depression and Dust Bowl. They would also contain stories of victories and accomplishments won by our earliest family immigrants from Norway and Wales. Most importantly, they would underline the timelessness of love, the kind of love that "bears all things, believes all things, hopes all things, endures all things" (1 Cor. 13:7)(NASB).

Maybe this story is for you. Possibly you have lost that sense of being loved. Perhaps a drought has visited your heart and laughter has not graced your face for quite some time. Do not give up because there's hope! Hope will not disappoint. Hope is the anchor that has held you, even while storms have tossed around turmoil and despair. Hope continues to hold you, and when your storms finally subside, a spectacular sunrise will greet you with a promise of a new day, fresh perspective, and laughter. And maybe, just maybe, a smile that brings life to your soul again!

QUESTIONS TO PONDER

1. What has been one of your more embarrassing moments?

2. Have laughter and joy subsided in your relationships with your spouse and/or loved ones? When was the last that time you laughed so hard that tears were running down your face?

3. Is your soul in a season of feast or famine?

11

FRANCISCO

Wrapped around Lake Okabena in southwest Minnesota is a surprising rural community called Worthington. On just one city block, you'll find neighbors from all kinds of countries like Ethiopia, Somalia, Guatemala, Mexico, and Laos. Signs in Worthington schools are posted in three languages: English, Spanish, and the exotic, curlicue Laotian language. If you're a foodie, you'd get a kick out of the world's cuisines jammed onto shelves in tiny ethnic grocery shops tucked among Americana Main Street stores. You could buy skewered grilled frogs on the way to mail your letters. Amazing.

Events are scheduled around the year to bridge some of the social and cultural gaps. Since it was autumn, a local family offered the use of their beautiful farm for a citywide fall festival complete with hayrides, pony rides, a barn dance, zip-line, and hog roast. My family and I were newbies, having just moved there to serve a local church. Besides being a total blast, the festival would be a great opportunity to meet a lot of people within in a short period of time, so we signed up to volunteer and headed out to the Kremer Farm.

While I was serving up sandwiches, a young Hispanic man

walked up to me with his hair all slicked back and tied in a ponytail. With a big smile, he introduced himself, "Hi! I'm Francisco!"

You know how there are people you meet in life and you just know there's something special about them? I knew in a moment that our lives would be connected. It was not much later that I came to realize Francisco's heart was just as big as his smile.

Over the next couple months, we bumped into Francisco, or "Frankie" as he was also known. I'd see him at church, usually in a big huddle of friends and neighbors. I'd see him dropping off or picking up his kids from school. Whenever I did see Frankie though, he seemed to be in the middle of doing something for someone else, and we didn't have tons of time for conversation until that December.

Ben, the youngest of our five sons, attended kindergarten in Worthington, and his first school Christmas program was like nothing we'd ever experienced before. There seemed to be a whole lot of risers for just the kindergarten class until they all started filing in from the back of the gymnasium. It turns out that there were five kindergarten classes in what was one of the largest elementary schools in the entire state of Minnesota.

I glanced at my wife. "Look! Ben is one of six Caucasians in the midst of eighty other five-year olds!"

It was so cool and so unexpected. Ben was among a minority in the rural Midwest. It really hit home with us in that joy-filled time of year that love, hearts, and smiles are common denominators, not skin color.

One of Francisco's kids, Mikey, happened to be in a kindergarten class too. After the concert, Frankie's whole family caught up to us with a special invitation. Francisco wanted to know if my wife Dawn might be willing to lead a children's choir for Spanish midnight mass a few weeks away.

She replied with a joyous, "Yes, of course! I would love to!"

I was thinking to myself, *How on earth is she going to pull this one off? She barely speaks any Spanish except for hola and gracias!*

She is not fluent in Spanish, yet she didn't let her inability separate her from Francisco's invitation.

On Christmas Eve, the church was arrayed with candles, sparkling lights, beautifully decorated trees, a nearly life-sized manager scene, and festive poinsettias across the entire altar.

Mass was to begin around ten o'clock that night. I say the word "around" because we discovered many Latino friends considered time to be a flexible, sliding kind of thing, definitely not the fixed, nonnegotiable kind of thing their Caucasian counterparts lived by. When you're invited to a function with your Latin American brothers and sisters, the best advice is to not stress out over when something was supposed to begin, most especially not when you think it was supposed to end.

I was really proud of my wife that night. Dawn figured out how the unfamiliar Spanish Christmas carols were meant to go and how to pronounce words she didn't know, and somehow she managed to pull off the whole choir director thing just fine. The celebration ended as beautifully as it began with sweet, brown-eyed and blue-eyed children singing "Silent Night."

It wasn't so silent afterwards! Every single worshipper present, from the youngest to the oldest, gathered in the church basement. We found to our amazement that the evening's festivities were only just getting started! Strangers became family, the serving platters were never empty, and language was no barrier to love.

Local musicians and members of a mariachi band had already played throughout the two-hour church service, and they continued to play at the Christmas celebration until after three in the morning.

We discovered on that holy night that our new community was like none other. Christmas among these people was all about family. Most were very young families with very few material possessions. They worked hard to provide the basic necessities for their daily lives, but when it came to gathering as one people in faith, each family seemed to pour out the entire contents of a special alabaster jar. These beautiful, selfless people offered all they had in celebration of the birth of Jesus. In addition to smiles and hugs, they offered stories of faith and triumph. They cooked, baked, and brought the best of everything they had to share with others. They offered love in spite of the slights they were commonly shown when their English failed. Each person present that night was welcomed, embraced, and shown a kindness that my wife and I had never before experienced.

On another night weeks later, Frankie passed along a message to us that some friends of his wanted to prepare us dinner as thanks for our helping with the ongoing children's choir. We were delighted to accept and racked our brains trying to come up with ideas of what to bring as a token of gratitude.

Frankie kept saying, "No. No. Please don't bring anything. You don't need to do that. Luís and Greta just want to honor their dinner guests."

So feeling a little awkward, my wife and I showed up at their house, thinking we were going to have a quaint Guatemalan meal with Luís, his beautiful wife Greta, and their adorable kids. As we walked up to the door, Dawn and I noticed all of the little ways this family showed their pride in having a place to call their own. Though the house itself was really tiny and had peeling paint, there were colorful planters beside the front door to hold summer flowers, Greta must have sewn the bright window curtains, and evidence of their deep faith could be seen in the special statuettes arranged between carefully tended plants.

A lovely little woman who was even smaller than my wife, who is five foot two, answered our knock at the door. She had an absolutely radiant smile and gave us each a gigantic hug, even though we were largely strangers to her.

Over her head, we could see that we were, in fact, only two of about twenty other dinner guests. A handful of people stormed the door to welcome us, including the man of the house, Luís. In a quick glance, I could see that everyone was somehow seated in that itty-bitty living room around a makeshift table, except Greta and Luís. Their delight was in making sure every plate was loaded with Greta's homemade tamales and rice and that their wineglasses were always full. I'm not even sure how they managed to create two more spots around the table, but they did, and we were absorbed into the family meal with effusive warmth and hospitality.

I would call Francisco my "happy little Franciscan." Even though he wasn't a professed religious monk or priest, his vows of simplicity, poverty, and humility were inspiring. He may not have known it when we began our friendship, but in a lot of ways, he was taking me along on a journey of awareness. Maybe my poverty was actually having stuff. Perhaps I had been seduced into thinking that I was rich.

Over the previous months, I had come to learn that simplicity creates a more welcoming environment and that humility is not a sign of weakness. Instead those virtues are signs of a heart that acknowledges greatness is not found in being the one, but pointing to the One.

It would be unfair and impossible to define a person using only one word, but if I had to try, I'd use the word "humble" to define Francisco. Who in his right mind would offer to watch someone else's five kids for ten days? Frankie. Who else would work on a broken-down vehicle stalled on the road in a miserable Minnesota blizzard? Frankie. The stories go on and on. Our family was only one of the many who were beneficiaries of this selfless man's generosity.

One day, Francisco called me up and was so excited that I could barely make out what he was saying. I eventually pieced together that an anonymous person offered him the opportunity to join a church group on pilgrimage and said that his travel expenses would be covered. It promised to be a journey of total discovery, one that would bring him to a place he'd likely never been on a map or in his heart. As excited as my new friend was, I could also sense some trepidation.

Because I'd been in a similar place on my life's journey, I recognized Frankie's reluctance to open up his heart to something new and unknown. I saw that his heart was also a bit ravaged by the circumstances of life. The broken pieces didn't fit back together in quite the same way they did before, and it could be a little scary to be vulnerable again.

Hearing both his joy and hesitation, I was reminded that, somewhere among the shards in each of our hearts, there is a voice. This voice welcomes us and offers a lovely space at his table. We're invited to dine with him and rediscover flavors we once enjoyed and to be challenged with new, unfamiliar seasonings as well. All we need to do is accept his invitation, and we'll be rewarded with inner peace, comfort, and a profound sense of belonging.

My wife and I had what we thought was a grand plan. Frankie gave me a key before he left on his ten-day pilgrimage so I could gather up the family's mail. Well, Dawn and I decided that, before Frankie got back, we'd tackle some of the projects we knew he started but never had time to finish. He was always sacrificing his needs for somebody else's. We only had about a week's worth of evenings to create Frankie's special surprise, so when Frankie's kids were situated with another family member, we dove right in.

When I unlocked Francisco's door for the first time, I realized how much he trusted me and valued our friendship. I also realized that we might have committed to a much bigger project than we originally planned. Simply put, Frankie's home was kind of a mess. Not a dirty or sloppy mess, not that at all. It was just super, super disorganized. It's a good thing that's my wife's specialty! She is married to me after all.

When I called her, Dawn said, "I'll be right over! Hang tight!" Some days I think that girl needs her own cape and theme song.

So for the next seven evenings, an odyssey of transformation was underway. Each room was being remodeled with love. Church members donated paint and painting supplies, bins and boxes to sort and store, brand-new bed linens, comforters, and curtains and rugs. Dawn and I had so much fun imagining Frankie coming home and snuggling up with his little kids to share stories of life and faith in rooms that bore witness to how much neighbors and friends loved their family.

The day of Francisco's return came quickly. Even though friends invited him to stay with them overnight, he decided that one more hour after the twenty-five he'd already traveled wouldn't make much difference. He said he just wanted to get home.

It was nearing the middle of the night when Francisco was finally dropped off at his place, having mentioned to mutual friends that he was dreading the chaos that awaited him after such an agonizingly long trip.

There was no way I was going to miss seeing the look on Frankie's face when he opened his front door, so I made arrangements to get there just before his arrival. Making a final inspection of all the rooms, I lit some candles and put them in the windows. Candles have always been such a source of comfort to me, representing warmth and peacefulness. It was my hope that the window candles would be the first indicator to Frankie that there was no darkness or disarray to fear in coming home.

Overwhelmed with sheer emotion, Francisco stood in the doorway to his home, dropped his suitcases to the floor, and allowed tears to run down his cheeks. He had arrived to a place where peace took up residency, where love covered every surface and wall, where order had been reestablished, and where the anchor of hope illuminated his home.

It would be a total understatement to say that our years serving that community changed our lives and our outlook. We learned a priceless lesson through the men, women, and children who found refuge there.

The lesson learned is one St. Terése the Little Flower puts best, "Small things. Great love."[3]

---

[3] St. Thérèse of Lisieux, *The Story of a Soul* (New York: Double Day, 2001).

QUESTIONS TO PONDER

1. We all have "Frankies" in our lives, friends who are sacrificially generous and selfless. Who are those people for you?

2. Greta and Luis extend their table of generosity to those of different colors, backgrounds, or ethnicities. Do you tend to do the same?

3. Do you hand over the key of vulnerability and transparency to those you love, or do you prefer to keep yourself locked up behind a false front?

12

HOME

One evening, I thought I'd spend a little time researching something I've always heard but never really verified for myself, that moving is the most stressful event in life after death and divorce. I literally spent hours scrolling through website after website. I read things on mental health sites, better living sites, and even travel sites. It blew me away that the super stress of moving didn't even make the top ten on most lists! And do you know why it blew me away? Because I was super stressed! We were moving again. I wasn't sure I'd survive it again.

The saving grace in our family is that my wife Dawn is really organized and has more of a type A personality. She gets stuff done. What works in our favor even more is the fact that she can brutally weed out anything that isn't used or practical and give it away. I've learned to just let her do her thing and serve as the grunt worker to haul loaded boxes or whatever. I'm definitely more of a type B kind of guy and easily get distracted. I kind of found that out the hard way.

While Dawn was pregnant with our first baby, I accepted the offer of a job in a town about four hours away. It promised to be a great bridge-building position serving two churches and a school as youth minister. Along with the job came the coolest apartment ever. Years before, when the educators in the school were mostly priests or nuns, they would use an apartment suite on an upper level of the school. That four-bedroom, two-bathroom apartment was offered to Dawn and me, and we were absolutely thrilled. It was going to be our first home as a new little family, our first move as a married couple, and the first time I ever dared to believe in a due date.

Dawn's ultrasounds predicted that our baby was going to be born in the third week of July that year, so I signed a contract to start my new job August 1. We let our landlord know we'd be out of our apartment on July 25 and started the process of getting things all packed up and ready to load into a self-drive moving truck.

My wife was a trooper. She had everything all ready for our baby and even sewed a whole nursery full of things I'd never even heard of: crib bumper, dust ruffle, and diaper caddy. On top of that, our entire apartment was packed into boxes except for one suitcase each and a baby bag for the hospital.

Dawn was so absorbed by getting our household ready that I decided to be helpful and do what I do best, spiritual stuff. Planning our baby's baptism was a real honor for me, and I gave it my very best effort. It was tough to decide on godparents, but we finally did. I got in touch with our home church and organized a baptism date and a priest. I outlined a menu for the reception afterward, lodging for guests, and some special commemorative prayer cards. Since I was really feeling joyful and charitable, I booked and paid for the perfect airline ticket for our baby's godfather.

There was just one small problem. There wasn't a baby yet. July 24 came, and there was no sign of labor starting. Thankfully, a dear friend came to our rescue and offered to let us stay with her until our child arrived. We were able to move out of our apartment on schedule. Another group of wonderful friends helped load up the moving truck, drive all of our stuff to our new place in the new town, and unload it all for us so I could stay back with Dawn, just in case. My wife and I watched the truck drive away, picked up the bags we kept for ourselves, and headed over to Janine's.

Janine's heart is huge, generous, and overwhelming. The place she lived was not. She called it her "hut," and that was the perfect description. There was a dinky kitchen, compact living area, one bedroom, and a miniscule bathroom. Since Dawn seemed about ready to burst, Janine offered us the use of her own bed, preferring to sleep on the couch. Fans were running in each little window, but they didn't do any good at all. We were in a nasty heat wave with temperatures way above 100 degrees for days on end.

After trying to get in and out of Janine's antique iron bed for nighttime bathroom visits, Dawn decided the living room floor was a better option and pretty much camped out there all day and all night for two weeks!

Poor Dawn, I knew she was miserable, and it was getting worse each day with the intense heat. By now, she was almost three weeks overdue. She finally had a meltdown. We were in a weird holding pattern wanting to get started in a new town, but not wanting a different doctor to deliver our child. I didn't want to make a big deal of it, but we were also getting real close to August 15, the date I set for the baptism! She begged her obstetrician to try an inducement.

A couple days later, a Friday, we were in the hospital, and Dawn was hooked up to the medicine that was supposed to help her labor begin. She had contractions that continued through the night, but only mildly. The next day, they tried it again all day. By nighttime, nothing significant was happening, and Dawn was exhausted. On the third day, both Dawn and our child were at risk, so full effort was given to help our little one's arrival. She was in labor all day and all night, and finally Joshua David Kinsman was born on Monday, August 9, at 5:05 a.m. He had to be born with help, and Dawn was in pretty rough shape.

Our awesome hospital provided a complimentary, candlelit steak dinner for new moms and dads, complete with wine for the daddy, who really needed it by then. As special as that was, it didn't do much to alleviate Dawn's pain and the 110-degree heat.

Trying to maneuver in Janine's boiling hot hut was challenging for my wife and son, so we knew we should try to make the four-hour drive to our new home. But don't forget! I planned the baptism, and we needed to get there first.

Dawn and I met in the church that both of our families attended in the same small South Dakota town. I proposed to her there, and we were married there. So I thought it would be extra meaningful for our first child to be baptized there too. When I was looking at possible dates, the fifteenth of August seemed best because it's a day when Mary, Jesus's mother, is honored, and it also happened to be my parents' wedding anniversary.

It's not necessary to go into all of the crazy details, but you'd get the picture if I said it was a defining moment in our marriage! It was a pretty rugged combination of things—people, chaos, sleeplessness, and pain—so we stayed a few days shorter than planned and drove to confront the mounds of boxes and household goods that were dumped off in our new home.

The beautiful people we are blessed to have in our lives took the boxes containing things we'd need right away and unpacked them for us. They even put together a bed for us and a nursery area for Joshua. That was move number one.

Now when Dawn and I were married, we said we'd really try to follow whatever God's plan was for us. We weren't going to lock ourselves into one community for our whole lives if we could be useful elsewhere. It was important for us to give our kids stability, but also to go where we were called. After that first move with baby Josh, we moved a total of three more times. The next two times were fairly easy because our boys were all young and Dawn was a stay-at-home mom. The last one though? It was a doozy.

Thanks to a hardworking realtor, our house in southwestern Minnesota sold quickly. We didn't end up having a whole lot of time to get ourselves ready to move to Milwaukee, Wisconsin.

It turned out to be a matter of weeks really. Since it was helpful to have found a buyer so quickly, we agreed to their choice of a closing date, even though it meant we'd have to be out sooner than expected.

The other minor issue was that my wife had a singing engagement during that time halfway around the globe in Bosnia and Herzegovina. After the closing papers were signed, she'd be on a plane, and our five boys and I would be on our own.

I really should have been paying a lot closer attention to how Dawn did things. She can look at chaos and make sense of it. She can sort it, label it, and stack it. I, on the other hand, was sworn in as Commander of Chaos. I create it, not fix it. I'm so ADD that I don't have the first clue of where to start. I also see why sane people pay movers to do it for them.

My strategic plan was to start with the two rooms in the back of our house, shove what I could fit into boxes, and then move to the next two rooms. Following this plan, we would wind up with all the boxes in our living room. It actually even worked out!

Dawn phoned to say she'd made it safely to Sarajevo. I answered from my queen bed mattress nest shared with five kids on the kitchen floor and said we were "awesome!" As we huddled there in our bare-bones home, the place we had called sanctuary for four years, I thought, *We must be crazy!*

I'm pretty sure I was anyway. One by one, the boys drifted off to sleep, while I lay awake in utter exhaustion, wrestling with emotions. We would be departing from dear friends, embarking on a move that would clearly take us much farther away from family.

Sometimes it's hard to own decisions that not only affect you but all those who are so very close to you. More often than not, change invites utter chaos. Chaos can be a messy, unpleasant experience, yet without it, nothing changes! My family and I were challenged to lean into all of the uncertainties that come with making a move: Do we live in the city or a suburb? Will we be able to afford a house? Is the new job going to work out? What about the schools? Will we all make good friends? How will the boys do in their new place?

A few days later, I watched as Dawn's plane made a final descent into Humphrey International Airport in the Twin Cities. My wife was finally home from her weeklong international trip. She was totally jet-lagged but energized enough to get the family rolling eastward.

I pulled into the driveway that was technically no longer ours, into the garage jammed with moving boxes. We were set to depart the very next day.

Our kids were all kinds of anxious about leaving, but one son was really having a hard time with it. Zach was struggling with leaving the community because he makes friends for life and really hates goodbyes. His cute, freckled face was pressed against the back window of our van, and tears of loss were streaming down his cheeks. All he knew and all who he knew would be gone with no guarantee of return. There was very little solace that Dawn or I could give him at this point. Zach was experiencing the now-familiar emotion of being separated from friends you love and who love you in return. Comforting each other, we continued down the road facing forward, accepting pain and excitement together.

Nothing brings quicker healing to the soul in times of transition than do joy and laughter. I'm happy to report that I supply a whole lot of both when I'm traveling with my family. See, for over twenty years, there's been a running joke about fast food and me. Not eating it, but ordering it. Just ask my wife and my boys. They've got enough of it recorded for me to be an international YouTube star.

You already know that I get easily distracted. You also already know that mine is a family of seven. What you might not know is that I have drive-thru performance anxiety. I don't care how many times I practice before I get up to the window. It totally doesn't matter if someone in the car has written out all of our orders in bright green crayon or has made cue cards for me. The thing is, when I actually get up to the window, I have complete loss of brain function. I stutter, I'm flustered, I can't speak or remember anything, and every single person in my car thinks it's the funniest thing on the planet!

On that day, they were all cracking up when a very calm, polite voice comes over the intercom, "Sir? Is anyone there? This is Amber. May I help you?"

"Just a second!" I croaked out and looked over at Dawn for help.

She looked back at me with her big, innocent, surprised eyes, and I heard behind me what sounded like a bunch of growling hungry cubs waiting to be nourished after a long winter's hibernation. All of a sudden, a wild uncontrollable laughter takes over. Even Amber lost it, and we could hear her laughing through the intercom system.

Dawn rolled out of the van to run into the restaurant to use the bathroom. I think it was probably more to escape the roaring laughter coming from the van. Either way, that moment changed our entire outlook. It was the moment that more accurately defined the adventure we were heading toward. It's that moment our family remembers more than the pain of pulling away from our former town. Laughter made all the difference in the world!

Just over seven hours later, a dear friend welcomed us into our new city of Milwaukee. It was he who extended an invitation to Dawn and me to embrace a journey that would demand every ounce of courage, trust, and faith.

As expected, the first years building an outreach ministry from scratch were incredibly tough. In fact, there seemed to be so much adversity that I began to doubt whether I really had it in me to do what the Lord was challenging me to do. What I did know was that I just needed to trust him and work even harder with the tools He gave me to use.

Completely out of the blue one day, I realized Dawn and I were actually physically living out a specific dream I'd had about fifteen years prior. Back then, I pictured Dawn and me walking down the streets of a quaint, Norman Rockwell-esque community. There were dogs walking their owners along a Main Street with lots of outdoor bistro tables and families looking at all of the window displays. The town had the appeal of history and tradition that had been upheld and cherished for generations. Holding Dawn's hand, I realized that our God is truly faithful. He gave us a dream, and we were living it.

More importantly, our family found something even far greater than a lovely physical place. We discovered a community of university students that would hold a very dear place in our hearts and be part of a vital, lasting legacy. In addition to the home that my wife, sons, and I occupied, there was another residence, a student outreach home.

When Dawn and I first began serving in ministry roles there, it seemed more like a building that needed a lot of love. It felt empty and neglected, without much warmth. Most of the people we met there adopted the traits of the building, as if love had been lost along the way.

Over time, we carefully rolled paint, tore up carpets, sanded floors, and added little homey touches that would encourage love to once again take up residence. The outreach home would be an inviting space where new students could enjoy a meal or a laugh. It would be where students would discover their worth and find healing. For many, it would become a home away from home where faith would be cultivated and celebrated.

Each and every heart longs for a home, and not one simply made with lumber, nails, or hammer. It is a home not shaped by blueprints or boundaries. It is not a structure representing confinement. I believe that what our hearts long for is quite the opposite, a place of freedom where dreams are unleashed, passions are fueled, risks are taken, and adventure is embraced. After all, you and I were imagined by love. We were created to love, and someday we will return to love. That's Who we call home.

QUESTIONS TO PONDER

1. More often than not, change invites chaos. Without chaos, nothing changes. What chaotic life event has produced the most significant amount of good in your life?

2. What events have you looked back on and made you marvel that you made it through them?

3. Maybe home is more of a mind-set and disposition of the heart than an actual place for you. Are you at home with yourself? Are you comfortable in your own skin? Or would you want to escape to a far-distant country?

13

HOW DID WE GET HERE?

What happens when a narcoleptic and an apnea sufferer undertake a ten-hour road trip? A disaster!

My friend Janine and I were going to travel by car to Denver, Colorado, for a conference. We both had work delays, so we got started on the trip much later than planned. Janine was exhausted from a long, tough week, and I'd been waking myself up a lot at night with sleep apnea, so we began the trip feeling tired. Thankfully, Janine manages fatigue better than I do and offered to take the first shift driving. Pretty simple, right? Not!

We were making that trip long before Siri and GPS, so I was chief navigator and kept the map in my hands for quick reference. It looked like we had only forty-two miles before we hit I-90 West. Once we got to that point, it would be smooth sailing with just one turn to take us to Colorado.

I relayed the plan to Janine. "Hey, it's a piece of cake. When you get to I-90, hang a right and head west."

She nodded. "No problem."

Janine is super smart. I knew she had everything under control, and in no time at all, I conked off to sleep. I had no clue how long I'd been asleep, but it must have been a deep rest because roaring thunder and big, fat raindrops pelting the roof of my car jolted me awake. There was an impressive display of lightning and torrential rain outside our windows. I was just taking in weather drama that seemed like the second coming when we passed by a road sign: "Brewster, Nebraska. Population 17." *What?!*

Somehow we wound up in the middle of Nowhere, Nebraska. I tore my glance away from the window and stared at Janine, who was completely baffled by my reaction. I couldn't help it. I started to belly laugh!

"What happened to taking one right turn onto I-90?"

Sheepishly, she said, "I really don't know. I think I missed a turn!"

That was just the beginning of a friendship that has always taken a slightly different route than the one most friendships take. In our case, it was literally the "road less traveled."[4]

It was Fat Tuesday, also known by most as Mardi Gras. Our church planned a dinner dance and costume party as a fund-raiser, so I called my buddy Janine and asked if she'd like to go with me. Since she and I both grew up in parochial school systems and kept in touch with our favorite educators, we had access to some pretty authentic outfits. "Father Dave" and "Sister Janine" came into existence, if only for an evening.

The church festivities wound down right at ten o'clock, but we were having such a blast with a large group of friends that we weren't ready to call it a night. When Sister Janine and I were asked to meet up with everyone down at the local saloon, we couldn't possibly refuse and clambered into our car headed for the Long Branch. That bar was really like walking onto a Wild West movie set. Most often, there was country music, line dancing, cowboy hats, fancy boots, and enormous, ostentatious belt buckles. The entire floor was covered with wood shavings that always reminded me of the stuff in a hamster's cage. The Western

---

[4] M. Scott Peck, *The Road Less Traveled* (1978).

theme was complete with a big, mirrored bar that ran the whole length of one wall.

On the night we went in costume, there happened to be a well-known cover band that was hugely popular. They were actually a big reason Janine and I looked forward to meeting our friends there.

As we blew into the Long Branch, we were greeted with laughs, smiles, and an occasional look of curiosity. It's not very often anyone sees a nun in full habit and a monk in priestly robes coming into a bar. Well, even Jesus liked a good party, and we were there to dance, not drink. Besides, people seemed to really be getting a kick out of our happy vibe.

Our group headed out to the dance floor right away, and almost as if the song were dedicated to Janine and me, the band started to play Norman Greenbaum's "Spirit in the Sky." It was a riot! Sister Janine genuinely looked like one of the nuns from *Sister Act*. The band's lead singer started shouting, "I have a friend in Jesus," and Sister Janine's arms flew up toward heaven doing a "holy wave" on the Long Branch dance floor.

Before we knew it, practically the entire saloon was out on the dance floor doing the holy wave too! It was so unplanned and so hilarious that the lead singer basically collapsed on stage, overcome with unrestrained laughter.

It was a night that we would never forget. Even thirty-some-odd years later, we still reminisce about it and laugh until our sides hurt! We look back on our crazy antics and say to each other, "How did we end up here?"

It seems like many, many more people ask themselves the same question, "How did we end up here?" I believe that I have discovered an answer to that. I realize there is a path, a road that, if taken, will lead us to trust. For Janine and me, it was growing a friendship that has endured the test of time.

"What was the test?" you might ask. It's trust. We trust that the Lord knows every hair on our heads, and because he cares for the smallest birds of the air, he will also care for us.

Through trust, we develop relationships that are truly life giving, and we're rewarded with a mutual understanding of true friendship. Janine and I have maintained such a true friendship because we care for each other and want the best for each other, no matter the circumstances. Relationships like ours that are rooted in faith and mutual respect are friendships that will last for all eternity.

Among the greatest gifts that Janine and I could give each other was time. We deeply valued our friendship but wanted to be patient and take time to figure out whether the friendship was meant to be something more. It really took a great deal of trust to communicate the longing of our hearts and be vulnerable enough to admit that our friendship was precious, but we were each being prepared for a future different spouse. Who would that person be?

Janine and I each had a string of previous relationships. We both also had a deep sense that we needed to be patient and trust in something or someone far greater than ourselves. We learned how to love without placing conditions on our relationship. As difficult as it may have seemed, that taught us how to truly love. In fact, what we learned affected the entire course of our lives.

Greg lived in the Black Hills of South Dakota. One night, he had a very distinct and memorable dream about a woman who was nearly his height of six feet tall. She had fair skin peppered with freckles and vivid hair that reached past her shoulder blades. In his dream, the woman had laughing eyes, and she was wearing a beautiful white gown with a train gracefully displayed around her ankles. She was so beautiful.

Behind the woman, he saw what looked like the inside of a basilica, and there was Native American artistry on the walls and ceiling. Greg could hear a Native American flute being played in the background. The entire scene was so peaceful and lovely. When he awoke, Greg recalled every detail of his dream with total clarity, and he allowed it to repeat in his mind over and over. It was a poignant dream that he would never forget.

Not long after the dream experience, Greg stood amid an excited gathering of about sixty-five people waiting at their departure gate at O'Hare International Airport in Chicago. He was just one member of a pilgrimage group about to board a plane destined for Sarajevo. They were on their way to a holy site nestled in the mountains of Bosnia and Herzegovina. Miraculously, the village community was unaffected by an atrocious and violent civil war.

Evidence of the Croatian War of Independence can be seen everywhere else in bombed-out buildings and burned-down homes. It has often been referred to as Europe's deadliest conflict since World War II. The hatred, ethnic cleansing, and inhumane war crimes are beyond what most people could ever fathom.

In the midst of this war-torn area of the world, there is a faith that could never be described in mere words. It is a faith seen on the faces of people who live there and visit there. As soon as you arrive in the small village, everything changes. There is something different, but it's nearly impossible to explain what it is. You sense a deep, abiding faith that has sprung up through trial, pain, and suffering and now shines as a beacon of hope to the world.

Among the many miracles that have happened in this oasis, my buddy Janine and Greg the dreamer met. There they were, halfway around the world, and settled in at an outdoor café enjoying coffee and balmy weather when they first met and got to know one another. I'm told it was as if each held a portion of a heart that perfectly matched the other's. Imagine how surprised they were when they found out that they joined the pilgrimage from different churches, but they lived in the very same South Dakota town! (Did I mention Janine has pale Irish skin, lots of freckles, and red hair that she wears long down her back? She's also six feet tall.)

Though Greg and Janine each lived in the Black Hills, Janine actually grew up on the Yankton Sioux Indian Reservation and attended a beautiful little church where she dreamed of one day sharing wedding vows with the man she married. The church, situated as it was on Sioux tribal land, was filled with breathtaking Native American artistry. Yes.

You see, there are dreams so real that they deposit hope. It's the same powerful kind of hope found in beautiful villagers' hearts in a faraway Bosnian community. This kind of hope eclipses adversity and brings expectation, amazement, and awe with it. It's a hope that creates reality from imagination. It is the kind of hope that once and for all answers the question, "How did we get here?"

QUESTIONS TO PONDER

1. Have you asked that question of yourself, "How did I get here?" Is it possible the roads you took in life led you in a different direction than what you originally intended?

2. How has your trust in God made a significant impact in the direction your life has taken?

3. Have there been dreams that have played out in the narrative of your life? How?

14

MANRESSA

I was just deciding whether to climb out of my warm, cozy cocoon into a crisp, early December morning when I heard my mobile buzzing on the nightstand. It was my baby sister, Annie. Through her tears, she tried to explain that our father's health had taken a turn for the worse and we should gather as a family to be with him.

There are many things that make a small town wonderful, and one of them is that you truly get to know those who live in your community. The physician who regularly treated my parents through the years became a friend to us kids, and we've always been deeply thankful for his guidance. It was Dr. Wilde's gentle suggestion to Annie that we do our best to hurry to our beloved father's bedside, for what could become his last moments with us.

As quickly as possible, I packed some basic necessities and slid behind the wheel for a ten-and-a-half-hour trek to my hometown. It was impossible for me not to recall the sadness and loss we children felt at my mother's passing. The many miles between Milwaukee and South Dakota seemed far too many, especially when I just wanted to be there. In hindsight, I see how those hours helped me prepare my heart to slowly accept the reality of what lay ahead, saying goodbye.

Praying for strength and peace, my son Zach and I quietly

approached my father's still form on the bed. Sensing our presence, he opened up his eyes just long enough to greet us with a half-smile. His smile seemed to have withered away with his body. Both at one time were bold, strong, and larger than life. Now though, it seemed that dementia and Alzheimer's chiseled away at my father's endearing smile and once-military physique.

As the illnesses advanced within my father, it became more obvious that our days of calling him up on the phone were over. All of us kids have a deep respect and love for our father and would dial him up whenever something popped into our heads that we wanted to talk to him about. Over time, the comfort I felt in hearing my father's voice was replaced with real concern about how anxious phone conversations seemed to make him.

And then conversations using words stopped. My father developed a new language. He would extend his hand out to us until we met his with our own. Then once safely there, he'd squeeze our hands, as if to let us know that he was so glad to see us. Even though my father could not make himself understood using words that, more often than not, would elude him anyway, he made sure that we knew we were loved!

I spent hours during the last days gently running my fingers through his hair. Reversing the way he held my hand as I child, I held his then, caressing the top in smooth circles to calm his fears and anxieties. It seemed like such a simple, profound way to return the humble strength my father showed to me in my lifetime. As I sat there, my fingers entwined with his, I reminisced.

The pain of a love lost had completely ravaged my twenty-year-old heart. I couldn't eat much or sleep well, so I sat at our family's kitchen table until I managed to doze off in the wee hours. I had fallen asleep with my head on my folded arms but woke to the homey sounds of cupboards opening and closing. It was my father. He knew something was troubling me, so he quietly came into the kitchen to make us both some coffee. The truly beautiful thing? He must have known I wasn't ready to try to put what I felt into words, so he just sat right next to me with his arm around my shoulders without saying a single thing. He recognized my longing to simply be loved and to love. You see, sometimes words, love, and hope can be best expressed in silence.

As I rested my cheek on the starched sheets of my father's hospital bed, I was reminded that Dad first introduced me to the mystery of silence. He invited me on my first silent retreat, a blessing I've sought each year since then, where my father and I journeyed together in inexpressible words of silence. We experienced an intimacy that few pursue and even fewer embrace. Seldom do others hear the invitation to quiet themselves because the world is clamoring for their attention.

Now having experienced the purity of silence, I feel compelled to share a similar invitation to all who are searching. Not only does silence reveal the world arrayed in utter beauty, it is also a vehicle that carries us toward vulnerability, transparency, and clarity.

My mind continued to scroll through years and memories set against the backdrop of Demontreville Retreat Center. It's a photo rolodex of treasured moments and shared embraces with my father. Among them is the retreat for which I was the designated bell ringer.

The bell ringer assignment came complete with a private bathroom and one's very own La-Z-Boy recliner in a room that overlooked Lake Elmo. Twice a day, the bell ringer gathered seventy men to prayer. I saw this task as a special privilege. I would be calling men to participate in a prayer not audible to the ears, but to the heart. To share such a journey with men I'd become friends with over a twenty-year span was a gift first offered so generously by my father. Initially I didn't quite understand its priceless value, probably because the packaging was rather unpretentious, much like my father.

For nearly three quarters of a century, the men of my family had prayed on the grounds of this retreat center. The legacy of their faith ran deep within my own veins. I was sure my Great-Grandpa Carroll would have never imagined that one day his great-great-grandchildren would be praying on the very same grounds that he did back in 1948.

My father and I were embracing a different kind of silence on that last day in the hospital. No words were spoken. They were, however, excruciatingly loud in my own heart. *If I could only hear him speak! If I could just bring him peace!*

Dad released a long breath, like a moan. In it, I heard a yearning for home, for rest. We children each longed to be nestled in his arms one last time, knowing that would be our final earthly embrace.

My face was mere inches from his, and I watched my father open his eyes with a fixed, distant gaze, as if he saw something far beyond what I could see. I knew he perceived something that we all hope for in this life, a hope that doesn't disappoint, a confidence to once again return to the one who loves and is love, a desire to return to those who have gone before us, awaiting our arrival.

Think for a moment, if you will, about what it means to arrive. Imagine a long, significant journey to a destination that some describe as magnificent but you've never seen. You're exhausted and empty as you approach the gate, but then rushing out of the door is the One who draws you into his arms in a warm embrace, saying, "Welcome home! Come rest. It is good that we are here" (Matt. 17:4)(NIV).

That's when we have truly arrived.

QUESTIONS TO PONDER

1. Sometimes words, love, and hope can be best expressed in silence. How have you experienced silence in your own life?

2. How comfortable are you with silence? Why or why not? Have you ever considered silence as a form of prayer?

3. What legacy do you hope to pass on to your children, grandchildren, and future generations?

15

LOVE WHISPERS

The fragrance of wood-burning fireplaces scented the crisp autumn air, and leaves crunched under my feet as I walked from my place toward Summit Avenue in St. Paul. I planned to spend an entire day on retreat at the Marry Hill Retreat Center. The retreat was advertised as "A Day of Reflection." To be honest, I wasn't sure what a twenty-four-year-old would reflect on other than that the Minnesota Twins were headed to the World Series!

In our initial group session, the retreat director invited us participants to reflect on the whispers of life. More specifically we were asked, "How have we heard the gentle whispers in our own lives?"

I thought, *Are you asking if I hear voices?* Well, let's just say we all have our mental playground of imaginary friends, but I wasn't altogether sure that I had heard whispers (other than my mother reminding me, "If you don't get the garbage out before your father comes home, you'll never hear the end of it!") What was being discussed wasn't making a whole lot of sense to me, and I was kind of relieved when it was time to break for lunch.

Around the table, I was hearing other men and women talking about the big moments when they were convinced they heard God. On one level, I knew it was possible, and since these were holy people, probable. But I eventually just tuned them out and tucked into the delicious tiramisu that was served up as a great finish to the meal.

Having some time to spare before our retreat began again, I excused myself from the group at the table and started to explore our retreat center. I marveled as I walked through the corridors of the 1903 mansion, thinking to myself how amazing it would be if the walls could speak. Imagine the stories that would be shared! Envision the luxurious dinner parties and black-tie dances. I mean, who has a three thousand-square-foot ballroom on one floor and a pool in the basement?

As I wandered through the estate, I passed a conservatory-type room where a grand piano stood pride of place in the very center. It was a deep, shiny mahogany, and the lid was propped open, revealing the intricate network of hammers and strings inside. I've always been intrigued by pianos, grand pianos in particular. On that day, my heart was captivated, and I felt pulled toward the piano by the sheer force of its presence. On that day, I heard a whisper, an actual, audible whisper, "Go play for me."

I know what you're thinking. Some other retreat participant was playing a joke on me. But I looked around, and no one was there. Interiorly, I felt drawn to go over to the grand piano and sit down to play. There were just two slight problems. First, there wasn't anyone nearby of whom I could ask permission. Second, I had absolutely no clue how to play.

I disregarded all of the manners my mother taught me and snuck closer until I was sitting on the bench, staring at a board full of black-and-white keys. Those keys meant nothing to me other than that they came in two colors and were in some kind of pattern. So what does someone do who is musically color-blind? He closes his eyes and lets his heart express its music.

Well, that's exactly what happened! I ended up playing for at least a half hour, having no clue, rhyme, or reason as to what I was playing. In spite of my lack of training, what emerged was truly beautiful.

My friend Monica passed by the conservatory as I was sitting on the bench and said, "Hey, I didn't know you played the piano!"

I looked at her and replied, "I don't."

"What do you mean? I just heard you, and it was gorgeous!"

"I have never played before," I tried to explain to Monica and told her about the whispered invitation to me to sit down and play. All I could tell her was, "It just ... happened."

Maybe, just maybe, God does whisper. Maybe our ears have become deaf to those longings within ourselves to create something beautiful. Not just for our own enjoyment, but to draw others through the beauty to its Creator.

A few years later, I was heading to the gym to recalibrate my day. For me, swimming has always been a favorite form of exercise. I don't have to put up with people grunting or making other assorted noises (if you know what I mean). Swimming always cleanses me of distractions. It's like my personal confessional without having to say a word. It's peace without interruption. While I exercise my body, my heart works through dreams and shortcomings, loves, and dislikes.

The gym and pool weren't very far from my home. At the earliest hours of the day, there's virtually no traffic, so I was kind of daydreaming and looking at the scenery as I drove. A semitruck pulling into the parking lot of our local grocery store caught my attention. On the truck's flatbed were pallets of softener salt, the kind that makes all of our showers in the morning pleasant.

Well, to my amazement and discomfort, I heard a gentle whisper, "Go! Go and thank this man for what he does."

Now my hands began to sweat, and my heart skipped a beat. I could only think to myself, *This is absurd! Who in his right mind would do this?*

So being a rational person, I let the whisper pass, and I proceeded to the gym. As I refocused on my route to the gym, I promised myself that, whenever I next saw a softener salt truck in the future, I'd respond. It seemed like a good bet. What was the likelihood of that happening again anyway? I considered myself to be off the hook, so to speak.

Months passed, and I had forgotten all about the salt semi and my promise. Guess what? I was awake in the early hours heading off to my gym to swim when I saw it, the semi with a flatbed of softener salt. *Of course.*

There it was again, sitting in the parking lot with the driver beginning to unload pallets of softener salt. That time, I couldn't dismiss the honest disturbance in my heart. So I pulled into the parking lot, fully aware that the guy was going to think I was an absolute fool!

I got out of my car, and he walked around the end of the semi trailer. *Here it is, Dave. The moment. Don't be a chicken!*

I said, "Sir, I just want to thank you for what you do. I see you come into our community without any fanfare and provide something we all need and we all probably take for granted. I'm not sure if anyone has thanked you, but I just wanted to say how much I appreciate you and what you do."

He looked at me with a deep gratitude in his eyes. "You're the first person in twenty-six years who has ever thanked me! Thank *you!*"

I suppose you're thinking to yourself right now, *Big deal, Dave. What's the significance?*

You see, there are people all around us each and every day who make our lives better and more comfortable without benefit of recognition or appreciation. They do what they do. Even when it may seem inconvenient or a bit uncomfortable, a whisperer is calling your name to take the initiative to love at what might be a most inconvenient time.

One morning, I was standing in line at our pharmacy to pick up a prescription. I swear I must have timed it exactly right because, as soon as I showed up, there was suddenly a long line. Patience isn't really my strong suit.

On that day, I happened to have our little two-year-old son, Ben, with me. I know that society generally judges two-year-olds to be "temperamental" or even "terrible." Ben was just the opposite. I think he was born with a smile, one that could melt the hearts of many.

The two of us were standing in line near an elderly man in a wheelchair. I noticed that a conversation of the eyes was taking place between Ben and that elderly man, so I picked up Ben and went over to introduce my friendly little boy and myself.

The man cheerfully responded, "Hi, I'm John!" John looked to be about eighty years of age and possessed an endearing grandfatherly smile that would warm any heart. He looked at me said, "Boy, would I like one of those."

At first I wasn't sure what John meant. I thought maybe there was something in a nearby aisle that captured his attention since Christmas was just around the corner. Our discussion was interrupted when the salesperson called my name, so I moved away from John toward the window to tend to business. While I was paying for my prescription, I noticed that Ben and John had their sights locked in on each other, both giggling and grinning. I'm not sure what conversation they were having that day, but their smiles said everything that needed to be stated.

As we prepared to leave the store, I wished John a "Merry Christmas," and he echoed the same back to Ben and me as we zipped up our coats and went on our way.

Pulling out of the parking lot, I was reminded of John's comment, "Boy, would I like one of those." It finally dawned on me what John truly wanted. He longed for the gift that was right next to me in the two-year-old bundle of smiles and joy. Maybe John and his wife weren't able to have children of their own. Perhaps John never even married. Possibly he had children but never knew what it was like to have a grandchild peck his cheek with a sticky kiss or snuggle in his arms to read a storybook.

I thought that maybe I should turn around and see if John were still at the store. Maybe I should invite John over to our home for Christmas. Perhaps I could set up opportunities to visit each other so both Ben and he could continue their conversation. As it happened, we continued on our way that morning, and I'm left to wonder what might have happened to all of those maybes if I'd listened to the whisper.

I am often reminded how important it is to pay attention to life's whispers. They may arrive more often than we think. The difference lies in whether we are willing to hear them and respond from our hearts. Perhaps the whisper is calling you to play piano in a symphony or to show gratitude to someone who makes your life more pleasant. Maybe a whisper can create a bridge of friendship between the very young and very old, bringing joy to the tired and smiles to the infirm. We'll never know until we hear the whisper.

Listen.

QUESTIONS TO PONDER

1. Have you heard a gentle whisper? How have you responded?

2. Do you feel you have become deaf to the whispers of God? Is it possible you have abandoned the longings of your heart to create something new and beautiful?

3. Have you felt like you heard a whisper but passed up on taking action, chalking up that whisper as a figment of your imagination?

16

UNFINISHED BUSINESS

Like most every kid in America, I couldn't wait for school to be over for the year so I could launch into all of my summer plans. My hometown was situated around a big pear-shaped lake, so on every decent day, my friends and I biked there to goof around on the beach and push each other around in the water. When we were tired of sand in our suits, we rode home to play kick the can or neighborhood-wide hide-and-seek. My own favorite game was red light/green light. I always managed to get to the finish line before everyone else, which appeased my competitive nature. Honestly, summers in Watertown were idyllic, and I have so many wonderful memories of growing up there.

But one of my fondest memories of South Dakota summertime was our family trip to Roy Lake State Park. Every June, our parents would load us six children and all of our stuff into our family's Plymouth Fury station wagon, which had a rear-facing third-row seat. How cool was that? My siblings and I had a take-no-prisoners rock-paper-scissors competition to see who would get to sit in the most coveted seat. These many years later, I'm still convinced the game was rigged. I never managed to win, and my two oldest sisters won every single time.

Roy Lake State Park is tucked into the northeast corner of

the state among centuries-old groves of trees. There are trails all through the park, campground areas, and various picnic sites. Roy Lake itself was dotted with all kinds of watercraft: paddleboats, fishing boats, and even some logs tied together, à la Swiss Family Robinson.

I remember what the park looked like, but to be honest, I don't recall where we slept or how all eight of us could possibly occupy a two-bedroom cabin for weeks at a time. Whenever one of us kids would complain about the tight space, Mom would remind us, "We would survive!"

And that was exactly what we did. For nearly a month, our family camped at Roy Lake with my mom's sister's family. They were a family of ten, so you can envision what a crew we were! My eight Tracy cousins would team up with my siblings and me for hours-long family softball games. Together we'd take big adventures all around the campground, usually ending with a Stewart's orange dream soda down at the lodge.

At nighttime, we'd look for twigs we could whittle down to roast hot dogs and marshmallows over the campfire. Smelling of mosquito repellent and kid sweat, we'd swap ghost stories under the stars.

The tough guys of the group would sneak off to capture the biggest night crawler worms for our fishing forays or to sell for candy at the bait shop. When we timed it right, we were able to hunt down frogs and crawdads, which our Aunt Ginny would cook up for us the next day.

Do you know that I don't remember eating a single thing that we brought to Ginny in a bucket? But I do know she made a mean homemade beef stroganoff. And that was light-years before it came packaged up in a box.

Our parents certainly knew something that we didn't understand at the time. It wasn't the hunt for crawdads and frogs, trips to the lodge, hours spent down on the beach, or our fishing expeditions. The best part about our time at Roy Lake was the simple fact that we were there together.

Not long ago, my cell phone jingled a tune I hadn't heard in a while. It was a unique tone belonging to my cousin Tim, one of the eight Tracy cousins I camped out with growing up. Many years had passed since our youth, but we'd always managed to stay in touch. I was delighted and surprised to see his name on the screen and answered his call right away.

"Hey, cuz!" he said. "For my birthday, my wife gave me a guided salmon fishing tour on Lake Michigan. Would you like to join us? Have you ever been salmon fishing before?"

All I could think at that moment was, *Lake Michigan is a big, deep body of water. It's beautiful to look at and stand beside, but crazy intimidating to be on top of!*

I tried to disguise my nervousness on the phone, but to no avail. The easy out was to simply reply, "Well, I'll talk to Dawn and make sure we don't have anything going on, and I'll get back to you ASAP."

Tim replied, "No hurry, Dave. It's only February, and the trip isn't until the first week in August. Call me back when you know."

Five months passed by, and I was still deliberating, except by that time I had a real good excuse. I had broken my kneecap not once, but twice that spring, and I was finally nearing the end of my recovery. Once again, I saw Tim's name lighting up my cell phone in rhythm with his special ringtone.

"Hi, Cousin Tim! How's it goin'?"

"Dave, we still have a spot for you on the boat, and we'd really love to have you join us."

I put my phone on mute to have a quick side conversation with my wife, wanting to ask her advice.

Dawn looked into my eyes. "Dave, when will this opportunity come your way again? Imagine spending two whole days on the water with your cousin. You love that guy!"

With no further hesitation, I touched unmute on my phone and exclaimed, "Sure, Tim! I'll see you on Thursday."

Needless to say, Tim's wife, Kathy, gifted her husband the most wonderful fishing expedition. Our salmon fishing trip was a massive success. Each of us four men caught one large fish per day. It can only be called beginner's luck because, for whatever reason, I managed to hook the largest salmon of all late on our second day, a nineteen-pound king salmon!

During our two days on the sixth-largest freshwater lake in the world, we shared the exhilarating experience of reeling in the unexpected. We watched sunrises kiss the horizon, as if to point us in the direction of our catch. We sat across from one another enjoying our meals, reminiscing on similar scents and flavors from our youthful days around a campfire.

I remembered my wife's encouraging question, "When will this opportunity come your way again?"

Her response seized my heart that day. "When?"

You see, over the past several years, my heart has been ravaged by the loss of loved ones: Mark, a classmate of mine who was married with twin girls that he loved so deeply; my brother-in-law Randy, who was known for his witty jokes during the holidays and who was a faithful husband and die-hard Green Bay Packers fan; and my older brother Paul, who had a brilliant intellect and the dry wit of Ron Swanson from the *Parks and Recreation* sitcom. All three of these dear men valiantly fought various forms of cancer, yet went home to the Lord long before any one of us were ready to let them go.

The word "when" doesn't necessarily promise a future. It is a word that collects a multitude of dreams yet to lived, adventures yet to be taken, and a pallet of moments yet to be tasted. "When" qualifies phrases like, "When I retire," "when I cash in that 401(k)," or "when I get the time," and the list goes on. I do not want to invite others to a life of irresponsibility. The fact of the matter is that the word "when" assumes a future. So I choose to invite others into the "now."

"Now" invites us to a life being lived. "Now" means tasting moments with the ones you love, celebrating birthdays, anniversaries, holidays, and the birth of grandchildren. "Now" means visiting the parent who resides in an assisted living center because his or her journey continues on a different path than before.

Maybe the "now" is nearer and more crucial than you think. Perhaps it's time to call that sibling who has shouldered the care of aging parents or reach out to a friend you haven't spoken to or visited in decades. Maybe your partner in life has been waiting to rekindle old memories and create new ones.

Several months ago, I was with some friends, enjoying the breathtaking beauty of the Pacific Ocean near Newport Beach. They happened to overhear that, even though I'd been to that region each of the past eight years, I had yet to swim in the ocean.

My buddy Mark grinned through his sunglasses and put his hands on his hips, asking, "Dave, when was the last time you did something for the first time?"

His posture proved that he meant business and was pretty much demanding an answer. Mark was challenging me to live in the now. He said, "Dave, answer me honestly. Have you ever taken a swim in the Pacific Ocean?"

The only answer I could possibly give him was, "No."

With zero hesitation, Mark proceeded to round up the rest of our band of brothers, Nino and Joe, and they all managed to surround me and forcefully propel me down the beach toward the churning water.

I'll admit, each time I stood in the sand at Newport Beach, I asked myself, "Why? Why haven't I taken a dive into these beautiful waters? What's holding me back from tasting something that's mere steps away?"

There was no more asking "why" or "when." My friends were

compelling me to live in the "now." The surf was up. The invitation had essentially been issued. So arm in arm, we all jumped into the waters and waded out toward the largest wave possible. We agreed that, when the biggest wave arrived, we would charge forward and plunge into the ocean with everything we had.

"Here it comes!"

Together, we surged forward, as if hearing our battle captain yell out, "Charge!" We were completely at the mercy of the wave's power and presence, hurling and plummeting us with ease, reminding us of something greater then ourselves.

One by one, we surfed the wave back toward shore, floating in the salty foam. We yelled out our elation and relief, knowing we did it! We may not have conquered the ocean's powerful waves, but we were immersed into the presence of the now. Through the coaxing of my good friends, I tasted something that I will never forget.

Now I ask you, "When was the last time you did something for the first time?" Let's choose to jump the fence of uncertainty and live life, one that is meant to be tasted and celebrated!

QUESTIONS TO PONDER

1. What childhood memories or family traditions have you held dear to your heart? How have they impacted you?

2. What opportunities have come your way and, because of your hesitancy, you missed a divine moment or opportunity?

3. When was the last time you did something for the first time? What was it? How did it make you feel?

17

WOODY'S ADVENTURE

Each of our sons is blessed with a personality that is uniquely his own. I can honestly say that parenting our five guys has been a blast because of how they've developed their own interests and talents.

As a little kid, our fourth son, Nathan, always seemed to be in the middle of exploring, creating, spilling, or decorating something, usually with the something he spilled. Nathan liked to retreat into his own imagination and his world, and we people in it were just characters in the adventure playing out in his mind. He'd take everyday things in his hands like socks and spatulas, and they'd be transformed into swords, rockets, horses, and helmets.

Nathan absolutely loved the Disney-Pixar movie *Toy Story* and had nearly every word in every scene memorized. His Grandma Mokey surprised him one day with a stuffed Sheriff Woody talking action figure, his favorite character. That toy Woody even had a pull string, which activated some of his famous movie quotes. Nathan would play for hours and hours, lost in the wonder of his vivid imagination.

One year, I happened to see a complete Sheriff Woody costume in Nathan's size. The full suit came accessorized with the same cowboy hat, vest, holster, and plastic gun that Nathan's toy action figure did. Oh my goodness! When I brought the outfit home and pulled it out of the shopping bag, Nathan's eyes lit up like a Fourth of July sky.

As he pulled the costume on, Nathan became transformed into the actual Woody. With each additional piece, our son fell more deeply into character. We marveled at our little guy's transformation. When everything was snapped and tied in place, Nathan was the toughest gunslinger in the neighborhood.

Now I have to say right here that, hard as he tried, Nathan was still more of a tender heart than a brave heart. He played the big, fierce dude pretty well, but he was intrinsically kind and gentle. Like most little boys, his desire was to have a bigger-than-life persona. With a kitchen mop, he was armed and dangerous. Crouched on a tree branch, he was a superhero who would swoop in and rescue a heroine from a nasty villain and carry her off to safety.

I happen to think that, when Nathan pictured the heroine in his imagination, she looked a whole lot like his neighborhood sweetheart, Peyton. Summer after summer, Peyton and her sidekick sister, Taylor, would show up on our doorstep at the crack of dawn. If they didn't show up at our place, you can be sure that Nathan was already knocking on their door.

Well, one beautiful Indian summer morning, Nathan decided to put on his brand-new Sheriff Woody outfit to impress Peyton. He waved to Dawn and me on the front patio as he headed down his usual path to Peyton's house three doors down.

My wife and I were enjoying our morning coffee, basking in the gorgeous morning, when the phone rang. It was our next-door neighbors, Dick and Carol, who we had adopted as honorary grandparents.

Interspersed with laughter, Dick told me that he just spotted Nathan headed down to Peyton's, but there was a minor problem. He had some fantastic accessories—cowboy hat, holster, gun, and boots—but that was it. He was wearing no clothes. Somehow, between our house and the next three, Nathan managed to lose the rest of his outfit. In other words, he was buck naked and completely unconcerned.

By the time I caught up with him, Nathan was already standing on Peyton's doorstep, and she was holding open her front door. A look of sheer embarrassment was on her face. Clearly oblivious, Nathan was planning to go into their house to play as usual. Super Dad intervened. I had him put on the shorts and shirt I carried along with me. It all worked out, except it did take a few days for the lost costume to materialize.

Each summer, I directed a discipleship camp for young people, the first week for middle school-aged students and the second week for high school students. Normally, D-camp, as we called it, took place at Lake Poinsett in South Dakota, but one particular year, I was persuaded to give the facilities in Estherville, Iowa, a try.

It was a new place and therefore a new adventure, so I invited Dawn and the four sons we had at the time—Joshua, Jonathan, Zachary, and Nathan—to tag along and enjoy the campground and lake as well. The boys were excited to be entertained by nearly one hundred students from all over the Midwest. My family and I occupied one of the cabins along the outer edge of the campground so the kids could have their fun without causing any distractions for the other campers.

It was actually a gorgeous location with a peninsula of land jutting out into the lake, causing the grounds to be surrounded on nearly all sides by water. This meant that people in the cabins dotted throughout the grounds all enjoyed a beautiful view of the lake. The main lodge, where we had our large group sessions, also overlooked the lake and was where we attended chapel and enjoyed our meals together.

There were countless opportunities for our kids to have adventures while they were there: hiking, swimming, archery, and tire swinging. It was the perfect place for Nathan's imagination to run wild. He brought his own favorite toys and props, but he also loved to dive into the big box of skit costumes my team brought along.

Each evening at camp, students, team leaders, chaperones, and my family would gather at the main lodge for prayer, devotional time, and mass. It was the perfect way to share stories about how everyone experienced God throughout the day and to go to off to our beds with joyful, grateful hearts.

As the days passed, hearts were anticipating what would be the week's highlight, the final night. Testimonies would be given, and relationships that had been building all week would be cemented. Through praise worship, and prayer, each person would stoke the fire in his or her heart that would ignite the faith of the community once he or she returned home.

It was just a short while before nightfall, and everyone was gathered in the main lodge, fully immersed in the worship music. Hearts and hands were raised, and a chorus of voices in unbridled passion filled the camp.

This is the setting into which my wife rushed with total panic in her eyes. She was set to play keyboard and sing with our group, but instead she headed directly for me and tried to communicate over the sound. All I could make out was, "Nathan."

I was looking at her, not understanding what she was trying to say.

She spoke even louder, "Nathan! He's not here! I can't find him anywhere!"

Nathan, always the adventurous type, would frequently wander off on his own in our home neighborhood, lost in his own imaginings. At this new, unfamiliar place, he was in terrible danger and wouldn't have known it. Water surrounded the camp, yes, but also with big rocks that were very exciting to climb. They could have drawn his attention. Worse, the dark of night was coming, and our time to find him was limited.

When it finally sank in that our son was in true danger, chapel time came to a screeching halt. Dawn asked all of us students and staff to help her find Nathan and quickly organized some search groups in different zones.

We all had a frantic fear, not wanting to imagine the worst, but knowing it may need to be faced. I just remember running over rocks and riffraff with my bare feet, yelling out our son's name. "Nathan! Nay-Nay!"

My heart was in my throat as I thought that our son might be lying lifeless, face-down in the lake water. Time was not on our side at all. Panic was written on the faces of all the campers and staff, and there was a distraught chorus of voices crying out Nathan's name with no response. Nothing can prepare you for a moment like this. Darkness had fallen, and the sweeping flashlights looked eerie and ominous.

Then we heard, "We found him! We found him! He's here!"

Every last searcher sprinted toward the voice yelling out from the main lodge doors. There sat Nathan on one of the pews, still groggy from being awakened. He must have come into the main lodge by the back entrance, nestled himself deeply under the skit costumes dumped out on the back pew, and was lulled to sleep by the prayer and music. When alerted, all of us searchers immediately began looking for him outside the lodge, out of fear that he was near the water. Nathan was oblivious to all that had transpired and sat there, sleepy and innocent.

My wife, overcome with emotion and relief, held our little one tightly to her chest as if it were the very day that he was born and she was seeing him for the first time.

The experience that night shook our family to the core. Handing over leadership to other team members, we left the students praying and praising in the chapel while we took our boys—Josh, Jonny, Zach, and Nathan—back to our cabin. Each of us was trembling with the fatigue that comes after an adrenaline rush. We were all overcome with such gratitude to God for protecting Nathan.

The next morning, Dawn stayed back at the cabin with Nathan. Both were exhausted and needing each other, so Josh, Jonny, Zach, and I headed up to the lodge's mess hall for breakfast.

As we walked, our oldest son, Josh, just seven years old, said, "Dad, you know this was going to happen."

I asked, "What do you mean, Josh?"

He said, "To teach us how to love."

It just stopped me in my tracks. How do you respond to that? To teach us how to love. What a lesson learned!

You know, more often than not, some of the greatest gifts in life are right next to us, and we don't even realize that until it's too late. Isn't that what we were placed on this earth to do? Love?

Life is too short not to love. We must ask ourselves, "How can we love? How have we overlooked those nearest to us and furthest from us? Why do we hold back?"

Lord, today teach us how to love!

QUESTIONS TO PONDER

1. Have you ever had a situation where you imagined the worst, yet your faith and trust kicked in despite the circumstances?

2. Have you ever lost someone or something? Did that experience move your heart toward gratitude?

3. What events in your life has God used to teach you how to love?

18

WHEN LIGHTNING STRIKES

My honey was taking a mini break from our little testosterone entourage to attend a friend's wedding about three hours from home. That meant I was on kid detail for a few days. No big deal, right? Our five sons were aged one-and-a-half years, eight years, nine years, eleven years, and twelve years old. (Okay, yes, it was a big deal.)

It always seemed that, when Mom was away, we boys would play. I'd basically set up a schedule that inevitably ended up going in a different direction than expected. I mean, what boy likes to color within the lines of a coloring book anyway? Certainly, none of mine did. Our boys were born with adventure in their hearts.

In addition to our sons, at least two or more boys from the neighborhood were hanging out at our house as well. Altogether the crew would unleash their energy and imagination throughout the whole neighborhood. When we were all goofing around in the yard, neighbors would pull their cars over to the curb and say, "Hey, Dave! I'm glad it's you and not me." Or "I don't know how you do it!"

I'd shrug it off like it was no big deal, but truthfully, I practically fell unconscious into bed at the end of the day. Don't tell my wife.

Friday nights are usually lots of fun, and that night with the boys and their friends was no exception. Pizza, popcorn, and pop were consumed in abundance, the kids were flying around like they were in a three-ring circus, and fun was had by all.

Typically when Dawn was gone, I'd let the boys watch movies until they couldn't stay awake anymore. But that night, I decided to change up the routine a bit and tucked them in their beds by 10:00 p.m. so we could all get a good night's sleep and play hard the next day.

Miraculously, the kids didn't complain or challenge my authority. Honestly, it was more like an act of God. I felt like a man who suddenly discovered that he had super powers! My wife and even the boys themselves would laugh at me when I tried to discipline over the years. Somehow they thought the face I thought was fierce was hilariously funny.

I'd growl, "Do you see this face? I meant what I said!"

Apparently my wife and children considered me to be more stand-up comedian than disciplinarian.

Saturday with our dude crew came really bright and early, thanks to the whole early-to-bed thing. I was up before the sunrise and had a gargantuan breakfast ready for the kids. It looked like I was feeding a mini army as they filed past the stove one by one, and I loaded up their plates with bacon, eggs, waffles, and fruit, the sleepover breakfast special. Typical boys, they scarfed their breakfast down in no time flat so they could all parade downstairs to zone out in front of Saturday morning cartoons.

I tucked our youngest son, Benjamin into his high chair to keep him contained while I tended to the mess the other boys left behind. Ben and I had our own goofy conversation going as I gathered up abandoned dishes and wiped down the table. Ben's giggle was so heartfelt and so genuine that it totally melted his father's heart.

I was placing the last of the breakfast plates in the dishwasher when there was an awful explosion. Flashes of light and bursts of smoke flew over my left shoulder. I felt myself suspended in midair, and time stood still. I vividly recall fixing my eyes on my little son Benjamin in his high chair and remember his eyes fixed only on me. I thought, *This is it. This is our final moment together in this life.*

My feet hit the floor, and I was jarred into disbelief that we were still alive. Then I heard the thumping feet of boys scrambling up the wooden steps from our basement, babbling incoherently in fear. All of us huddled together in the place where, just moments before, we enjoyed a hearty breakfast together. We held each other in amazement that our peace could so quickly turn to panic.

Shock wore off enough for me to take inventory and see that all the boys were present and accounted for. Shortly afterward I was able to determine that, on an early Saturday morning in May, we had all survived a lightning strike. The blasts of light and smoke I saw were markers of the force of lightning that struck a tree about seventy-five feet from our front door. All but one of the windows on the east side of our home were shattered into jagged pieces of glass.

In fact, the lightning strike was so powerful that, in addition to destroying our house windows, windshields of cars parked along the streets were shattered, and clumps of grass and dirt were thrown blocks away. Family photos and knickknacks were knocked off people's living room walls and shelves miles away. We'd hear for months that residents of our small town said it was the loudest blast they'd ever experienced, and they believed the lightning strike must have transpired in their very own backyards.

We were at ground zero that morning. The lightning bolt hit our tree mere yards away on the boulevard. Had our sons not been put to bed earlier than usual Friday night, they would have still been snuggled asleep at the moment shards of glass shredded their bed coverings. I shudder to think what would have happened to our dear boys.

While our friends Pat and Lisa helped to clean up the disaster lightning had wrought, I noticed a terrible ringing in my right ear. I also noticed a breathtaking miracle that happened that morning. The only pane of glass that wasn't disintegrated by the blast was the one that my son Ben and I were standing in front of. It was the only one.

I have always kept the perspective that the devastation could have been so much worse. I had actually been up early enough that I thought I'd mow the lawn. It was Mother's Day after all. Dawn was expected back, and I would have loved to welcome her home to an immaculately kept house and tidy yard. Had I been out mowing that morning, I wouldn't be alive today. And since Ben would have been in his baby carrier, neither would he.

In the moment of crisis, Benjamin fixed his eyes on me. I still marvel at the fact that, in spite of the chaos that erupted in the matter of an instant, Ben focused his eyes on me. Ben's response was mirrored on mine. He did not demand to be comforted. He simply looked at me and based his response on how I was reacting. I believed that the Lord, in his goodness, would keep me safe, and without saying a word, Ben believed it too.

What I've come to realize from that day to this is that babies will become boys, boys will become men, and men will become fathers. Whether we like it or not, they will mirror the lives we represent. They will respond to their adversities in the same way they've witnessed their fathers responding to adversity. They will father in the way we father. They will love their brides in the same way we love our brides.

It's been a very short time since I've said goodbye to my father. It's painful to not be able to call upon the one who has so generously mirrored for all of us children qualities that we would attribute to him. I vividly recall the day I realized that I would never be able to phone my father and the home he represented because Alzheimer's disease and dementia had taken up residence within him.

Now it was our time to mirror, to hold his hand, to comfort the one who had comforted us for a lifetime. One of the greatest honors we can bestow upon those who have loved us from birth is to love, to forgive, to be generous, to serve, and to cherish those we call family.

My father, a first lieutenant in the army, was given a military interment honoring his service. It was a day very much etched upon my heart, never having experienced a military interment before. I was awestruck hearing "Taps" being played, watching the soldiers methodically, and, with great honor, ceremonially folding the flag.

On one knee, a soldier presented my father's casket flag to my sister, the next of kin, after my brother's passing. It was a powerful exchange. We were all within touching distance of Laurie and felt the impact of the moment very deeply. Then without any hesitation, Laurie took the precious flag, turned toward me, and then placed the flag in my lap, saying, "This is for you, Dave. You are the patriarch now."

A flood of emotion overcame me that day. It took me by surprise, much like the lightning strike. But what was birthed that afternoon was an exchange, an entrustment to become a father who would reflect Christ to his two nephews, the nephews who had each lost a father much too early in life.

I would also mirror Christ to the five boys I have been entrusted with, who will someday become fathers themselves. Maybe, just maybe, they will view their father in much the same way as Ben on the day of the lightning strike that Mother's Day weekend.

This invites us all to ponder the legacy that we will one day pass on to our children. What will be said of us? What stories will be told? Those into whom we've made deposits of faith will speak one day. And what will they say?

The flag has been placed in your lap. The exchange has happened. Your legacy matters.

QUESTIONS TO PONDER

1. How might we live our life differently if we knew it was quickly coming to an end?

2. My son Ben fixed his eyes on his father during the lightning strike explosion and wasn't shaken by the outward circumstances. Do you recall a memory of an event that took you by utter surprise and you were given the grace to respond in a faith-filled way?

3. Much like the honor of a flag placed in my lap, each of us is entrusted with a legacy. What legacy will you pass on to your children?

19

THE RETURN

It's the beginning of a new semester at the University of Wisconsin-Milwaukee, and my sidekick in life, Dawn, and I are preparing for the autumn's incoming students. We had prepared all summer for what would be our first year of outreach to the UWM student body.

A somewhat scraggly, slender student walked into my office, which was situated at the very entrance of the student center. The young man reminded me of the middle-school students we coaxed awake and drove home after a sleepover at our house. Let's just say that, by all appearances, style and presentation were not on the top of his list. I thought to myself, *Haha! What a character!*

He looked at me and said, "Hey, I'm Nino!"

"Nino? You're the first Nino I've ever met! Where did you get that name?"

"Well, I was named after my Grandfather Nino Antinucci."

"So you're Sicilian!"

He looked at me as though I'd just spoken a crime against humanity. "No, I am Italian. Don't ever let my mom hear you say that! You'd you never hear the end of it."

From that day forward, ours would become a very endearing relationship.

One of the primary goals that my wife and I set before us

in our campus outreach at UWM was to find two students who would become the face of the place that all who visited would call their "home away from home." We envisioned having two individuals, one male and one female student, who would lead the way in hospitality, service, and love. We waited and watched the movement of students during the fall semester.

With his gift for music, Nino joined our worship group for student services on Sunday mornings. I have to laugh because Nino would roll in on Sunday mornings, true to himself, wearing shoes that were not a matching pair and hair that hadn't known a comb since the morning before.

I had begun to notice a young woman who was consistently coming to student events and our Sunday liturgy. She seemed to radiate such an inner confidence and beauty. So after our 10:30 a.m. service, I walked over to where she was standing at the back of the chapel to introduce myself.

"Hello! I'm Dave."

She appeared a bit timid, not quite sure what I was going say, and then responded, "I'm Amy."

"Say, I've seen you around the student center a lot." Then without holding anything back, I continued, "I would like to invest in you as a leader. I think you could have a tremendous impact on the lives of the students here at the UWM."

I paused, and tears began to trickle down her face. I wasn't sure at first what had stirred such profound emotion.

Amy gathered herself with a sigh and then looked at me with an unpretentious smile, saying, "Yes!"

I saw such a sigh of relief in her eyes. It was as if my invitation validated what was stirring in her heart. I said, "Amy, I think you will have a tremendous impact on the lives of so many students, but I don't think you can do it alone. It's so important that you have someone walk with you for support and encouragement. Better together than alone, right?"

She smiled with such gratitude and said, "You don't know much this means to me!"

"You're welcome, but it's not about me. It's about how can we make this place a home, a home away from home." I then said, "Hey, can I introduce you to someone?"

"Sure!"

So I brought her to the front of the chapel near the worship area. "Amy, this is Nino."

Amy had a huge smile on her face, as if she had just been introduced to a stand-up comic waiting to give the punch line to a joke.

Nino, looking like a schoolboy trying to muster up enough confidence to ask her to dance, responded in his typical nutty way, "Hey there! I'm Nino!"

Amy smiled and laughed, and so began the journey of two students who transformed the fabric of the place we called the Newman Center. Both Nino and Amy were pursuing majors that would allow them to be leaders at the Newman Center for five years. It was an extraordinary opportunity for all of us to develop lifelong friendships with them. Their mutual friendship was also quite an example to many.

Before we launched each new season, I asked Nino and Amy if they felt they could continue on serving at the Newman Center, and both always agreed with a resounding "Yes!"

Each year in early spring, I would take a few students out with me to a leadership conference in Irvine, California. The conference would be a catalyst for them to dream, create, innovate, and inspire other students. It would expand their vision of what could possibly be.

It was always such a joy to share this experience with them. However, our trip wasn't merely to attend the conference. It was also an opportunity for me to spend quality time with the students and for them to solidify relationships with one another. It was about allowing conversations to take place.

Year after year, we looked forward to a special tradition. The students and I would jump into our rental car bright and early the day after the conference concluded and enjoy a mini road trip. We'd take a drive down to Newport Beach from Irvine along the beautiful Pacific Coast Highway, spending all morning and afternoon taking in a final feast for the senses. The road trip would conclude a week certain to be etched in our hearts forever.

Throughout the years, I have made a commitment to the students that I would take a stroll down the beach with each one of them for an hour or so. Nino was first.

As we walked, the warmth and subtle breeze reflected a picture-perfect day. In my mind, I rehearsed again the conversation that was about to unfold. The day had finally arrived for me to move the words from my brain to my mouth.

"Nino?"

"Yeah?"

"Amy."

"Yeah."

"Have you ever thought ..."

Nino paused and then said, "We're too good of friends! That would be weird!"

Then he relayed to me a conversation that he had with his father just prior to our trip to California. They were out one Saturday morning for breakfast and his dad asked Nino the same question, "Have you ever thought of dating Amy?"

Nino responded, "Dad, I can't date my best friend!"

His father exclaimed, "You millennials have it all wrong! That's exactly who you want to marry. You want to marry your best friend!"

The story of Nino and Amy continues to be written, and the witness of their goofy, growing love reminds us to return.

Return to what? We are asked to return to our first love, to do the things we did at first. You see, life brings about deposits of sediments, which can impede upon a love that once was bursting with life. Sediments come in all forms, such as the loss of loved ones, financial struggles, health issues, the raising of one's family, and loss of employment, and the list goes on.

Can love go on? Can it bear the erosion of what was once so pure, delicate, sacred, and holy? I am convinced the answer to that question is a definitive "Yes!"

In the book of Revelation, John writes a letter to the faithful in an ancient Greek port city of Ephesus, which was on the coast of Ionia, three kilometers southwest of present-day Selçuk, Turkey. It was a highly influential center of travel and commerce with over 250,000 inhabitants. Three major Roman trade routes were running through Ephesus, and because of the excellent port location, it was a vital trade-link city for transporting goods such as olive oil, marble, iron, and gold from the West to the Asian interior.

Over time and bit by bit, sediment was allowed to build up in the port harbor, to the point of filling it in completely. In these modern days, it's difficult to believe that Ephesus was not only great at one time, but it was a port city. What's left of Ephesus now lies six miles inland! The area around the former thriving city and harbor turned into a mosquito-laden swamp. In fact, a series of malaria epidemics decimated the population, and within one hundred years, most inhabitants abandoned the city.[5]

Our hearts could suffer the same fate as Ephesus unless we are vigilant. If the port to our heart becomes calloused and the cracks are filled with fear, betrayal, rejection, or sadness, the pathway into our heart will be impenetrable.

An anchor of hope is calling us to return. It is the same anchor found in John's letter to Ephesus in the book of Revelation. "I also know that you are enduring patiently and bearing up for the sake of my name, and that you have not grown weary. But I have this

---

[5] http://www.patheos.com/blogs/markdroberts/series/ancient-ephesus-and-the-new-testament; http://www.ephesus.us/ephesus/port_of_ephesus.htm.

against you, that you have abandoned the love you had at first" (Rev. 2:3–4)(NASBCE).

I'm reminded that our hearts, when they are open, offer a limitless potential for love, meaning, significance, and purpose. When we remain open to those possibilities, our lives are vibrant and growing, full of life.

Remember the moment you experienced falling in love for the first time and an awestruck, reckless, all-consuming focus on the other person consumed you? Such is the type of heart John challenges us to possess and pursue.

Like Ephesus, it would be easy to allow silt and sediment to build up so slowly over time that you don't even realize that the distance between you and the object of your love has grown much too wide.

Return! Return to your first love. Do the things you did at first. Hold her hand, and be reminded of the very first time you dared to take her hand in your own. Kiss her and bring to mind the place and the moment where you shared your very first kiss together. Write a letter, reminiscing on how you felt the very first time you saw her. Remember the instant you saw your bride for the first time, arrayed in a breathtaking gown that reflected both her beauty and the beauty of her Creator.

The sacred beckons all of us. You and I who are in danger of becoming a living Ephesus, return! Return to hope because hope never disappoints. Return to love because love never fails! (1 Cor. 13:8)(NASBCE).

QUESTIONS TO PONDER

1. What sediments have impeded upon your most treasured friendships or relationships?

2. What initiatives have you taken to restore those relationships?

3. "Do the things you did at first." As you were falling in love with another person, what were the specific things you chose to do that expressed how deeply you felt toward him or her? Do you continue to express your feelings in the same way today?

20

WHAT'S IN THE NAME?

It seemed that, with each mile, winter winds intensified, hurtling sheets of wet snowflakes across our windshield. The weatherman promised a bad storm was on its way through the Midwest, but my two oldest sons and I decided to brave our road trip regardless. We packed the necessary items in my car's back seat: blankets, candles, matches, shovel, and winter gear. And we took turns pushing toward our destination. We would be traveling ten-plus hours through the Wisconsin, Minnesota, and South Dakota winter for what would be one of the most memorable Christmas gatherings of our lives. The first stop on our adventure was in the rural town where I grew up. Josh, Jonny, and I were blessed to spend Christmas Eve with my father Earle at his assisted living facility.

As we arrived at his room, my father greeted us with a smile and a sigh of relief. He may not have known precisely who we were, but he immediately recognized that we were dear to him and that we loved him very much.

That evening, I was reminded of a statement my mother made to us six children. She said that, if she were to precede our father in death, we must be certain that we didn't leave him alone. It occurred to me that we children took our mother's words to heart and all did our level best to be with our father as frequently as we could.

My mother loved and served my father so graciously. If anyone knew my father's needs, it was my mother. Her love for my father would echo through her children, well beyond her earthly time with us. I believe she would have been proud of our care for our father throughout his final years.

During our stay with Dad, I hoped for a moment when his memory was clear so I could ask him a question I'd been meaning to ask him for years. I always wondered why my parents gave my older brother Paul his middle name. What story or person was behind Paul Stewart? If anything, you'd think my brother would have at least known. He apparently didn't.

My father shared with my sons and me on Christmas Eve that Stewart was one of his closest friends in the military. As matter of fact, after one tour was complete, Stewart tried to convince my father to reenlist for another four years of service to our country. My mom was mere months from giving birth to their firstborn, so he declined the request.

Steward reenlisted anyway, and shortly after he did, the Korean War broke out. Not long afterward, my father was notified that Stewart, his friend/comrade/brother, never survived the war. He paid the ultimate sacrifice for his country. So in honor of his dear friend, my father gave his eldest son the middle name Stewart.

We had many long conversations about history and family, and we were saddened that our time with Dad passed so quickly. After an emotional farewell, Josh, Jonny, and I once again loaded up the car to continue on our trek.

We were driving still further west to South Dakota's capitol, where my brother Paul and his family lived. The boys and I were buckled in and just taking off on the three-hour journey when Paul called my mobile. Knowing that my sons and I considered him to be a genius chef, Paul was excited to share over the speaker phone what he had planned for our arrival dinner.

Our mouths had already begun to water, and it was definitely torturous to have to wait hours before enjoying what promised to be a spectacular meal. My brother Paul loved to cook because he loved, period. He very much enjoyed putting time and effort into the feast that we'd be sharing together. Yeah, I'm guessing what some of you might be thinking, *Well, Dave, it's just a meal!*

But it wasn't just another meal. It would one of the few remaining meals prepared by Paul that I would ever have the privilege to enjoy. You see, Paul had been valiantly fighting cancer for years at that time and was fearlessly facing eminent death. Those of us present knew it was our last Christmas with him. We were eating the last meals and sharing the last conversations. We were holding each other in the last embraces on this side of eternity.

You see, when we sit at table, it's an encounter. It isn't simply about partaking in a beautiful feast prepared with love, but the beautiful feast sets the stage for our souls to encounter intimacy. Time and dedication was given to crafting the food. Even more time and dedication was given to crafting our spoken words. You see, at Paul's table, we were savoring words that would become memories only love could create. Love is a language that, for many, has been abandoned along with meals around the table.

My brother Paul and I learned special life lessons from one of the best teachers ever, our mother Connie. Seasoning every family gathering was a unique family flavoring, one that always made Mom's feasts so very pleasing to our palates. Her table was always set with thoughtfulness and her own special something at everyday meals and every holiday meal. That seasoning was love. Love changes the very atmosphere. Love changes all that we taste, not only at the table but in every interaction with family, friends, and strangers as well.

Relaxing around Paul's table that Christmas, I asked my

brother if he had ever asked why he had been given the middle name Stewart. Amazingly he said, "No."

So I proceeded to tell him about the story about our father's friend, a comrade, a man that Paul never knew. Even so, he mirrored his namesake in a lot of ways. Like my father's friend, Paul was loyal, faithful, dedicated, and hardworking. Paul would do what needed to be done for the sake of honor, even though his commitment may go unnoticed or unrecognized.

How appropriate it was that, while we were still gathered around Paul's table, there was a friendly shout from the back door.

The governor of South Dakota and his first lady were welcomed into the family home and comfortably seated with us around the dining room table. Unbeknownst to us, the governor had asked to visit Paul for a couple hours that weekend, and I'm so grateful that our time overlapped so my two sons and I could witness a beautiful tribute. That evening, in the presence of family who loved him so deeply, my dear brother was awarded the first-ever "South Dakota Servant Leadership Award."

Paul was one who never sought to draw attention to himself, instead choosing to quietly give the best he was to others. The honor given to him that night mirrored the name given to him at birth, Paul Stewart, for a friend whose sacrifices have changed the landscape of a country and for a servant who has changed the landscape of a state.

We too have been given a name, a life, and an opportunity to change the landscape of the communities in which we live. We are given opportunities to impact the lives of our friends, families, and those of people we may never personally know.

What will those opportunities look like? What will they taste like? I do not know. But what I do know is this. When service is seasoned with love, it changes everything. Many will ask what the secret recipe is, but few will take the time necessary to discover its true flavor and meaning.

The South Dakota winter day dawned crisp and white, and

we carefully loaded our vehicle for the long trip back home. It was time to say our farewells. We struggled to say goodbye to a brother, an uncle, a friend, and a servant who was embarking upon his own journey. Paul would soon be moving forward with the love and support of many, but it was a journey that he had to ultimately travel alone.

I remember that morning as Paul and I embraced each other for the last time, that our two souls were immersed in a loving, brotherly embrace. We knew beyond doubt that, as much as we relished our earthy meals together, the banquet we'd one day share together would be beyond belief!

QUESTIONS TO PONDER

1. When you think of a name, whose comes to mind first? What qualities or attributes come to mind when you think of that name?

2. List the names of those who have had the most significant impact on your life. I suggest writing a note to those top three on your list to let them know how much they have contributed to your life.

3. What are your fondest memories as you recall family meals throughout the years? Were there any unique traditions around the family table? Have the traditions continued?

21

TAKE ME WITH YOU

It was my own personal dream car, a 1985 Mazda RX-7 with a rich gold exterior paint set off by bold black trim and shiny chrome. I could vaguely see a spot or two where I missed rubbing off the wax from my weekly detailing session. The RX-7's interior was just as showy with its soft black leather seats and faux wood inlay on the dashboard. The car's two seats were slung low to the ground, but the sky was literally the limit when I cranked open the moonroof. I mean, I realize I was a pretty nice guy in my own right, but the car made me hugely popular. It brought me an almost silly joy to tuck myself in behind the wheel to run lame errands. It was an all-consuming joy to be able to drive myself to speaking engagements.

The American theologian, Frederick Buechner wrote, "The place God calls you to is the place where your deep gladness and the world's deep hunger meet."[6]

Speaking into others' lives is definitely that sweet spot for me. I savor speaking to middle schoolers who always seem to be juiced up on caffeine prior to my arrival. I relish speaking to high school students who are trying to figure out the direction that their lives will take post-graduation. I revel in speaking to college students

---

[6] Frederick Buechner, *Wishful Thinking: A Seeker's ABC's* (HarperCollins, 1993).

who are living on their own for the first time and tasting a freedom they've never experienced before. I delight in speaking to those of any age who are ready to unleash their creativity and passions. And I truly love speaking to souls in assisted living centers and nursing homes who are longing to hear a voice of optimism offered with smiles, laughter, and, most importantly, a hug, a kiss, and a hand held.

One particular morning, I topped off my coffee thermos and jumped in my car for the day's adventure. I was scheduled to speak at a daylong high school retreat. So my car and I were chasing off to our destination while the sun began to rise over the South Dakota plains.

Vast open fields stretch for miles and miles, so when the sun crests up over the horizon, it opens up what looks like a sea of land. It is simply magical, breathtaking, seeing the expansive prairie landscape. The brilliant sunrise illuminated crops that stretched farther than I could see inevitably making me wonder what the first settlers must have seen. I imagine their awe when they first set eyes on the promise of South Dakota's rich soil and fragrant grasses.

I was lost in my thoughts and captivated by the landscape when my heart started to race. It was such an unusual thing for me that I admit I was kind of shocked and then really concerned. I thought, *This is it! I am having a heart attack!*

I couldn't seem to get a breath, and my hands felt wet and clammy. Before I knew it, an uncontrollable panic set it. There I was, out in the middle of no-man's-land with at least thirty miles between my current location and anything that might resemble civilization.

Not having a clue about what else to do, I whipped my Mazda RX-7 around 180 degrees, as if I were a stunt driver filming for the *Fast and the Furious*. Thank God there were brick-sized cell phones way back then. The only problem was the scarcity of cell phone towers out where I was driving. I would be lucky to have bars enough to make an SOS call.

There was one bar flickering on and off, but I prayed it would be sufficient and called my honey, Dawn. Trying to control my shaky hands enough to press the little buttons, I dialed her up. It rang once, twice, and then three times. By this point, I was certain my time on earth was up and I was going to die alone. It rang again. *No answer. She must be getting ready for work or still sleeping.*

It rang a fifth time.

"Hey, good morning, honey!" she said.

"Dawn! I don't know what's happening. My heart is racing, and I think I'm going to die! I don't know what to do."

She began to pray out loud over the phone while I was trying to focus in on what she was saying. Minutes passed, and my heart slowly regained a bit of regularity. Each breath started to come a little deeper, and I felt less like I was hyperventilating. I listened to Dawn's soothing words of encouragement.

Finally I was able to regain my composure and tell her my location. I wound up only about fifteen minutes from home. Even so, I didn't think I could make it back to our place without her help. She said she'd get to me as quickly as she could and stated that I should continue to calmly pray until she got there.

Little did I know with that first episode, I'd be repeatedly dealing with similar bouts of travel anxiety for the next several years. My life would be entirely defined by the word "if." "I'd love to come to visit you *if* I can drive the whole way myself." Or "I'll only drive five miles so help can get to me *if* I have a heart attack." I was experiencing something that research teams around the world have been studying and effectively treating, anxiety disorder.

Even though I felt like I was taking my last breath on earth and my heart was a beat away from stopping, in reality, I was suffering an anxiety attack. The attack kicked in the same type of adrenaline rush one would experience in a catastrophic event. For example, if you saw someone about to be crushed under a car, you'd suddenly have a surge of strength enough to lift the car completely off the victim.

My wife and I found a beautiful tape recording of Philippians 4:6 set to music, "Do not be anxious about anything …" (Phil. 4:6–9)(NRSVCE). When I felt an episode coming on while I was in the car, I'd pop it in right away. It was certainly calming and helpful to pray and meditate on God's Word and to believe in his promises. Eventually I also shared my concerns with our general practitioner. In addition to daily prayer, my doctor added alprazolam.

As difficult as it was at first to accept that medicine was needed, I realized that my doctor's treatment plan helped to change my life's focus from "if" to "when." It's somewhat telling that, now in 2017, 50 million prescriptions for Xanax (or its generic form, alprazolam) are written each year. That's more than one prescription per second. Go figure.

I was sitting in one of the back pews for a 7:00 a.m. weekday mass, trying to decide whether I should go on retreat and work through what was going on in my life. I felt like God had totally abandoned my once jovial, fun-loving self. "What happened to me? Who am I? Did I cause this anxiety? Did God allow it as a sort of retribution for my shortcomings?"

My attention was diverted off my own musings back to the mass I was attending. I heard my dear friend, the priest, praying words from the liturgy, "And Lord free us from all anxiety as we wait in joyful hope."

"Wait? How long, O Lord?"

Let's just say that waiting is not my strong suit in life, and it certainly isn't a popular trend in our society. In fact, if we live to the age of about eighty, we will spend at least five years of our lives waiting.[7] We wait in grocery lines, in a drive-thru, for a

---

[7] https://www.thefactsite.com/2010/03/how-much-time-people-spend-doing-stuff.html

premiere to start, in traffic, outside an emergency room, on the couch expecting a timely return of teenagers before curfew, and so on. You get the point. We wait a lot. Maybe our society has evoked a lifestyle that promotes impatience.

I've already admitted that patience is not my strong suit. I'll confess though, I have even more of a struggle with silence. My wife is usually the one waiting for me to be silent. I immerse myself in conversations with anyone and everyone each minute of the day, it seems. It brings me a great deal of joy to talk with people. It follows then that silence would be a challenge. Difficult as it is, I have experienced amazing blessings moving from the "chaotic" to the "still."

Hearing the priest's words that day at mass inspired me to take some time out of my stressful life and slow down enough to hear God's voice. So before long, I found myself on my own personal retreat. It was where I would spend several days moving from everyday life distractions to a place of prayer. Belgian writer, Louis Évely, described it this way, "The prayer that still remains unheard is not our prayer to God, but His prayer to us."[8] It was my goal to cease my questions and my loud prayers asking God for his help and just listen for the voice that might have something to say to me.

As it happens, I unknowingly scheduled my retreat on a weekend featuring a leader who suffered anxiety in much the same way. That priest became a valued companion who chose to journey with me. Through compassion and friendship, he helped me maneuver through the minefield of "if" statements.

For me, that minefield was bleak and scary. It is not usually a place I'd ever want someone else to find me in. It's not a comfortable place to be. I had to walk carefully around emotional bombs like insecurity, belonging, and worth. I was looking for footholds to

---

[8] Louis Évely, *In His Presence* (Burns & Oates Ltd, 1970).

prove that I was cherished and loved in spite of my anxiety and fear.

Not only did Father Rice meet me there, he helped me learn to navigate through it all until I came out on the other side. "Hi! I'm Father Dick Rice! It's so good that you are here. Welcome!"

I felt like there was such a kindred spirit between us the very first moment we met. It was if our journeys mirrored each other's. The more Father Rice spoke, the more I was convinced that I was there on that weekend for a very specific reason.

In a moment of immense vulnerability, Father Rice shared with us gathered men how he viewed himself. He said that, throughout his life, he considered himself to be very stingy with his possessions to the point of sinfulness. In truth, he was not at all stingy, but a voice of shame, over time, convinced him that he was.

God allowed Father Rice to have a dream in which he perceived himself in a completely different way. In that scene, Father Rice saw himself on a mountain, arms overflowing with loaves and fishes. The Master was tenderly looking at him, reminding Father Rice that his life had, in fact, been one of great generosity and that he, through his selfless actions, had fed the multitudes.

Before releasing us from the large group gathering into a silent meal and then a time of personal prayer, Father Rice invited each of us men to ponder what narrative we saw ourselves in. His invitation made me inexplicably restless. When the bells finally chimed for breakfast, I was relieved to adjourn to the dining area to eat. Each of us men sits at the same table every year as means of becoming more acclimated and well disposed to making a great retreat. This plan also removes any need for thought or feelings of awkwardness. It's a simple way of allowing us to focus on our journeys and learn to live in the moment.

The spot I had occupied for years was next to a large window overlooking the retreat grounds. During our meals, the retreat director selected soft music to play or podcasts of some great spiritual writers to learn from as we dined. As I was admiring the view through the window, a beautiful song began to play with the lyrics, "Be still and know that I am God."

Tears began to stream down my cheeks. I sensed that God was finding me and I him. Thoughts flooded through my mind, *Where can I go from your Spirit?* (Ps. 139:7)(NRSVCE).

I heard in my heart the narrative of the lost sheep. *God, I am lost! Will you find me? Will I be found by you? What will your response be when you find me? Will accusations be rendered and shortcomings revealed? Will your Shepherd's voice be full of anger and disappointment?*

The song concluded. Afterward we stood for a prayer of gratitude for all the men who had made retreats at Demontreville and for all those who would one day come. It was time to exit the dining hall, and I began to walk the lush grounds, still pondering my sense of being lost.

The path I was walking led up a hill, and at the top, I was surprised to find a Carmelite monastery. I began to weep again. *Was God finding me?*

It seemed so easy to get lost in the busy world and forget who and what we were supposed to become. The Demontreville Carmelites are hermits who seek prayer and silence, stillness, and solitude. In some ways, their daily lives were the opposite of mine.

Tolling bells interrupted my musings, and I made my way back down the hill to our chapel. The moment we men got settled in our seats and were quietly focused, Father Rice entered.

He opened that session with prayer, inviting us to reflect on the passage of Scripture he was about to share. Following the prayer, Father Rice spoke of our heavenly Shepherd who leaves the ninety-nine and goes after "the one." He spoke of the Shepherd calling us his "little ones" and that "there are angels in heaven always looking upon the face of their heavenly Father."

Father Dick continued to read to us that "the Good Shepherd

leaves the ninety-nine to search for the one ... and if he finds it ..."
(Matt. 18:12–13)(NRSVCE).

My heart nearly stopped! *I can't have a Shepherd that might find me. If? If he finds me? That doesn't give me any assurance of being found. I desperately need to be found!*

Father Dick concluded his reflection with a closing prayer and shared that he'd be available afterward for spiritual direction. With that, he genuflected before the altar and left the chapel. Frantically I jumped up from my seat and followed right behind him. As soon as Father Rice sat in his chair in the counseling space, I closed the door behind us and practically collapsed in front of him, burdened with my overwhelming sense of being lost.

I said, "I'm really struggling with the scripture you read. It said *if* the Shepherd finds the lost sheep. That's it? That word has already crippled me!"

Father Rice looked at me with the same deep sense of affection that a Shepherd would have for his sheep and said, "Dave, read Luke 15:2–5. You have your Bible. Open it up, and I want you to read that passage to me."

It said,

> And the Pharisees and the scribes were grumbling and saying, "This fellow welcomes sinners and eats with them." So he told them this parable: "Which one of you, having a hundred sheep and losing one of them, does not leave the ninety-nine in the wilderness and go after the one that is lost until he finds it? When he has found it, he lays it on his shoulders and rejoices" (Luke 15:2–5) (NRSVCE).

"See, Dave?" Father Rice said to me. "*Until* he finds it. *When* he has found it."

There are no "if" statements. The Shepherd finds me. Not

only does he find me, he puts me upon his shoulders and rejoices. Intimacy is felt; identity is restored. His voice is heard!

It's true that the word "if" defined my life for a while, but I believe that, in many ways, there has been a purpose in it all. When I first suffered anxiety attacks driving off to speaking engagements here and there, I saw them as weakness and a marked lack of trust.

In truth, my illness caused me to seek God and lean on him in a way I would never have done, if I relied on my own abilities instead. The messages I deliver have a whole new depth and transparency, and I understand better what others have journeyed through too.

You see, being comfortable can be just as debilitating as the word "if." We should ask ourselves, "Am I willing to risk being lost? Am I willing to lean into the unknown to find the known God?"

As a matter of fact, when I consider "the ninety-nine," I feel deep sadness for them because they may never experience the intimacy of being sought, lifted up, and shouldered with great rejoicing.

As I packed up to leave that life-changing, illuminating, and healing retreat, Father Rice looked at me and said, "Take me with you."

I hadn't heard that expression before, but now I understand, and I ask you to do the same. "Take me with you." I hope that whatever you have captured from my stories has moved you, inspired you, or brought a smile to your face. Take that with you. Take me with you.

QUESTIONS TO PONDER

1. How has the word "if" affected your life?

2. Meditate on the following scripture from Philippians 4:6–7 (NASB):

   Do not be anxious about anything, but in every situation, by prayer and petition, with thanksgiving, present your requests to God. And the peace of God, which transcends all understanding will guard your hearts and minds in Christ Jesus.

   How has God worked in and through your struggles with anxiety?

3. Read Luke 15:1–7. Where do you see yourself in the narrative of the Parable of the Lost Sheep? Would you be among the ninety-nine in the safety of your community, or are you one who was placed on the shoulders of the Shepherd "with great joy"? What has been your most intimate experience with the Shepherd?

CONNECT WITH DAVE

These days, you see the slogan a lot: *"Better together than alone."* I look back at my life and realize how blessed I have been to have had the parents, family, teachers, coaches, friends who have had a significant impact on my journey. They poured life into me. They inspired me to become more than what I thought or imagined. They taught me life lessons that have carried me through some of life's most challenging circumstances. You see, I believe life is best lived within the context of community. As a matter of fact, I believe God does some of his greatest work in community. I often think of the "Parable of the Paralytic Man." It took a community of four men to pick up the paralyzed man from his mat, cut an opening on the top of a thatched roof, and lower him down into the presence of the One Who could restore not only his body, but his soul.

The same is true for us. Connecting with one another brings about Life! When we take time to reconnect within the context of Community, God shows up! Faith is infused, Hope is restored and Love transforms. I would love to have the opportunity to connect with you and your community. If you would like me to speak at your event, campus, church or conference feel free to contact me at info@davekinsman.com.

Follow me on: DaveKinsman.com, Facebook and Instagram
You can order my book on Amazon and Barnes & Noble.
Make sure you add your rating and reviews on Goodreads
Book Club (discounted rates available)

85496697R00093

Made in the USA
Lexington, KY
01 April 2018